Skunks, Bogies, Silent Hounds, and the Flying Fish

The Gulf of Tonkin Mystery, 2-4 August 1964

Robert J. Hanyok

Contents

Publishing Information

- Nimble Books LLC: The AI Lab for Book-Lovers
- Fred Zimmerman, Editor
- *Humans and AI making books richer, more diverse, and more surprising*
- (c) 2024 Nimble Books LLC
- ISBN: 9781608883394
- Nimble Books LLC ~ NimbleBooks.com

Bibliographic Key Phrases

Gulf of Tonkin Incident; 1964; SIGINT; NSA; Vietnam War; US Navy; North Vietnam; Cryptologic History; President Johnson; Robert McNamara;

Publisher's Note

The Vietnam War continues to cast a long shadow over American history and the world's understanding of international relations. The debate about its origins and how it escalated has raged for decades, fueled by conflicting narratives and a lingering distrust of official accounts. This document, a declassified and previously un-published account of the Gulf of Tonkin Incident of 1964, goes deep inside the National Security Agency's (NSA) signals intelligence (SIGINT) operation during the crisis, revealing a shocking truth: the second attack, which was used to justify a congressional resolution granting President Johnson a blank check for military intervention in Vietnam, never happened.

This article first published in the NSA *Cryptologic Quarterly* and drawing on an unprecedented amount of newly-released and previously unavailable SIGINT data, analyzes the events that transpired between August 2-4, 1964, revealing how analytic errors and deliberate misrepresentations of intercepted communications ultimately led to a tragic escalation of the conflict. Using detailed analysis of the raw SIGINT reports, this document exposes a previously hidden dimension of the Tonkin Gulf Incident, highlighting the complexities and potential pitfalls of signals intelligence analysis. It is a must-read for researchers, policymakers, practitioners, and anyone interested in understanding the origins and dynamics of the Vietnam War. This document offers a rare and compelling glimpse into the inner workings of the NSA, revealing the potential for human bias and error within even the most advanced intelligence agencies.

With intelligence warning and attribution playing an ever-more-central role in conflict, deep understanding of its pitfalls is essential reading.

Truth in Publishing: Disclosures

**This article is a fascinating deep dive into the Gulf of Tonkin Incident, a pivotal event that helped escalate the Vietnam War. It's packed with details, but be warned: it's also about as exciting as a bureaucratic meeting.*.

Strengths:

- **The author has access to a treasure trove of never-before-seen SIGINT material, providing a fresh and detailed perspective on the event.** You won't find this level of detail anywhere else.
- **The article meticulously debunks the "official" version of the story, revealing how the Johnson Administration manipulated intelligence to justify its actions.** It's a classic case of "truth is the first casualty."
- **It's written by a former NSA analyst, lending an air of insider authority to the narrative.** If you're looking for an unbiased account, this is probably not the place to start.

Weaknesses:

- **The writing is dense, detailed, and, frankly, dry.** Think of it like reading a particularly dry textbook on naval warfare. You'll be thankful for that strong coffee.
- **The over-reliance on technical jargon and military acronyms is overwhelming for the average reader.** You'll probably need a glossary of terms handy, or at least a good dose of Google.
- **The author gets bogged down in the minutiae of signals intelligence, making it hard to stay engaged in the narrative.** If you're hoping for a thrilling spy story, this won't deliver.

Overall: This is an essential piece of historical scholarship, shedding important light on a significant event. But be prepared for a grueling journey through dense prose and technical details. Bring your reading glasses, your caffeine, and maybe a dictionary – you'll need them all.

Analytic Table of Contents

Introduction: The Origins of an Intelligence Failure

The Gulf of Tonkin Incident of August 1964 as a defining moment in the escalation of the Vietnam War. A reassessment of the event through newly uncovered classified materials. The Johnson administration's use of the incident to secure the Gulf of Tonkin Resolution. The importance of SIGINT in shaping the administration's response to the events of 4 August.

The Desoto Patrol and Operation Plan 34A

The role of SIGINT in supporting the two American programs. A review of the Desoto missions' origins. The dual mission of the Desoto patrols to assert freedom of navigation and to collect intelligence. The expansion of the Desoto program in the waters of Southeast Asia.

The OPLAN 34A missions

A review of the objectives and tactics used in the OPLAN 34A. A look at the American strategy of escalation of the war through graduated response. The four levels of OPLAN 34A. The reasons for continuing the commando raids in spite of their failure to achieve their objectives.

The 2 August Engagement

The events leading up to the attack. A detailed account of the communications activity of both the U.S. Navy and the DRV. The identification of the "enemy" by the Americans. The mixed reactions by the Johnson administration to the attack. A review of the SIGINT activities during the day of 2 August. A look at the command, control, communications, and intelligence (C31) system of the DRV.

The "Uneventful" Day, 3 August

The continued tracking of the two American destroyers. The salvage operation conducted by the DRV. An examination of the communication between the DRV Navy and its shore-based commands. The activities of the 34A mission.

The 4 August Incident

A review of the "official" version of the 4 August engagement. The initial reporting by the Marine contingent at Phu Bai. The interpretation of the DRV communications as a planned attack. The role of radar and sonar in the incident. The arrival of American aircraft.

The "Attack" Message

An examination of the first "attack message" from the Marine contingent at Phu Bai. A review of the problems with the translation. The alternate meaning of the Vietnamese phrase for "military operations." A look at the reaction by the American destroyers.

The "After-Action" Report

A critical examination of the NSA translation of the "after-action" report. An examination of the problems with the translation. A comparison of the San Miguel and NSA translations. The confusion surrounding the identities of the Vietnamese callwords. The file time of the message.

The Silent Dogs of the Night

A look at the lack of DRV naval communications or radar emissions during the incident. An examination of the absence of attack C3I. The lack of other intercepts to support the claim of an attack. The role of the 34A mission on the night of 4 August.

The "Del Lang Chronology"

The chronology as an "official" record of the events. A review of the problems with the chronology. The selection of SIGINT products. The absence of critical information. A look at the reporting by the NSG. The absence of any mention of the attack in North Vietnamese communications.

The 18 September "Attack"

A review of the September incident. The actions of the destroyers, the USS Morton and the USS Richard S. Edwards. The North Vietnamese response. An examination of the available SIGINT.

The Aftermath

A review of the aftermath of the incident. The passage of the Gulf of Tonkin Resolution. The role of the incident in shaping the course of the Vietnam War.

Conclusion: The Ghost of the Gulf of Tonkin

The legacy of the Gulf of Tonkin Incident. The incident as a defining moment in the history of U.S.-Vietnamese relations. A final assessment of the role of SIGINT in the incident.

Abstracts

TLDR (three words)

Gulf of Tonkin lie

ELI5

This is a story about a time when American ships were in the water near Vietnam. The American ships thought that Vietnamese boats were going to attack them, but they were actually just trying to fix the boats that got hurt in an earlier fight. The American ships fired on the Vietnamese boats, and then the Americans told everyone that the Vietnamese had attacked them first. This wasn't really true, but the Americans used it as an excuse to start a war in Vietnam.

Scientific-Style Abstract

This article examines the role of signals intelligence (SIGINT) in the Gulf of Tonkin incidents of 2-4 August 1964, which led to the Gulf of Tonkin Resolution and escalated US involvement in the Vietnam War. Through a meticulous analysis of newly declassified SIGINT records, the author presents a compelling case that the second attack on US destroyers on 4 August was fabricated. The analysis reveals that: 1) the initial "attack" order was misinterpreted, as the North Vietnamese boats were involved in salvage operations, not an attack; 2) no command and control communications consistent with an attack were intercepted; 3) a key "after-action" report was fabricated by combining two unrelated intercepts; and 4) a substantial amount of SIGINT evidence contradicting the attack narrative was omitted from official reports and chronologies. The author concludes that NSA personnel deliberately skewed SIGINT evidence to support the narrative of a North Vietnamese attack, illustrating the potential for misinterpretations and manipulation within the intelligence community during times of crisis.

For Complete Idiots Only

Context: This is about some super secret stuff, like how the U.S. spies on other countries.

The Story: We're talking about a super important event, the Gulf of Tonkin incident. It's a big deal because it kinda got the U.S. into the Vietnam War.

What supposedly happened: The U.S. had some boats in the Gulf of Tonkin, which is a body of water off of Vietnam. These boats were spying on the Vietnamese, but they said they were just there to show off their freedom to sail around.

The U.S. claimed the Vietnamese attacked the boats twice.

The Truth: Turns out, there was probably only one attack. And the second one? It never happened.

What really happened: The Vietnamese were actually just trying to fix their broken boats from the first attack.

How this all happened: The U.S. spies, who are called cryptologists, got their facts wrong. They misinterpreted what they were hearing on the radio and thought the Vietnamese were going to attack.

The Aftermath: The U.S. got really mad and bombed the Vietnamese. The event led to a resolution in Congress that basically gave the president the power to do whatever he wanted in Vietnam.

So, what did we learn? The U.S. government lied to the public. They used spies to get the information they wanted, not necessarily the truth.

Think of it like this: Imagine you have a friend who's always trying to tell you what to do. They're not your friend, they're a spy. And they're telling you things that aren't true to get you to do what they want.

That's kinda what happened in the Gulf of Tonkin.

Learning Aids

Mnemonic (acronym)

DRVS

Damaged **R**epairs **V**ery **S**ensitive

Mnemonic (speakable)

Attack **D**oubts **R**adars **V**ery **S**uspect

Mnemonic (singable)

The Ballad of the Boats

The DRV has a problem, their ships are badly beat. T-333 and T-336 are taking on some water. The Maddox is sailing around and Hanoi wants to know. What are those "Skunks" and "Bogies," and where are the "Boats" going to go? It's all a big mystery, and the evidence is thin. The boats are in for repairs, and Hanoi wants to win.

Excerpts

Most Important Passages

"The Gulf of Tonkin incidents of 2 to 4 August 1964 have come to loom over the subsequent American engagement in Indochina. The incidents, principally the second one of 4 August, led to the approval of the Gulf of Tonkin Resolution by the U.S. Congress, which handed President Johnson the carte blanche charter he had wanted for future intervention in Southeast Asia. From this point on, the American policy and programs would dominate the course of the Indochina War. At the height of the American involvement, over a half million U.S. soldiers, sailors, airmen, and marines would be stationed there. The war would spread across the border into Cambodia and escalate in Laos. Thailand assumed a greater importance as a base for supporting the military effort, especially for the air war, but also for SIGINT purposes of intercept and direction finding." (Page 1)

"The second finding pertains to the handling of the SIGINT material related to the Gulf of Tonkin by individuals at NSA Beginning with the period of the crisis in early August, into the days of the immediate aftermath, and continuing into October 1964, SIGINT information was presented in such a manner as to preclude responsible decisionmakers in the Johnson administration from having the complete and objective narrative of events of 4 August 1964. Instead, only SIGINT that supported the claim that the communists had attacked the two destroyers was given to administration officials." (Page 3)

"The major operational components of OPLAN 34A were airborne operations that inserted intelligence and commando teams into North Vietnam, and maritime operations (MAROPS) which consisted of hit-and-run raids on coastal installations and facilities. These latter missions were known under the operational title Timberwork. The teams were made up of mostly South Vietnamese Special Forces, known as Luc Luong Dae Biet or Biet Kich, with some foreign mercenaries (mostly Chinese and Koreans) to crew the attack craft. The American involvement, though extensive in the planning, training, and logistics portions, was minimized to achieve the usual "nonattribution" status in case the raids were publicized by the North. No Americans were allowed to participate in the actual raids." (Page 8)

"At 2140G (1440Z), Herrick informed CINCPACFLT that he had commenced firing on the attacking PT boat. The Turner Joy had begun firing at its return shortly before this. Both destroyers had a difficult time holding a radar lock on their targets. Within five minutes, the return on Maddox's radar, which was moving away from the destroyers, disappeared from its screen at a distance of about 9,000 yards. The one that the Turner Joy was tracking kept approaching, and at a distance of about 4,000 yards, it disappeared as well." (Page 23)

"The sonar returns of the supposed torpedo attacks were later determined to be a result of the high-speed maneuvering by both U.S. ships. As we saw above, the first "evidence" of a torpedo launch by the enemy boats came from radar. When one of the radar tracks turned away to the south from a westerly heading, this was interpreted by the Americans as a torpedo launch. The sonar rooms in both destroyers were then alerted to a possible torpedo attack. Four crewmen aboard the Turner Joy thought they saw a "white streak" in the water as the ship turned. Both vessels had then gone into wild evasive maneuvers to avoid the torpedoes that were thought to have been launched against them. It was this high-speed gyrating by the American warships through the waters that created all of the additional sonar reports of more torpedoes. Every time one of the destroyers changed course, the sonar reported the distinctive high-speed sounds of torpedoes. Eventually, Herrick and the other officers realized what was happening: the rudders of the two ships had caused the high-speed returns when they reflected the turbulence of the ships' own propellers." (Page 24)

"The Johnson administration used the 4 August incident to ride the resurrected resolution, now popularly referred to as the Tonkin Gulf Resolution, through the Senate, with only two dissenting votes. It was portrayed as a moderating measure "calculated to prevent the spread of war." 193 However, President Johnson now had the legal cover to use whatever military force he wanted. When he heard of its passage by both houses, he laughed and told an aide that the resolution "was like Grandma's nightshirt. It covers everything." 194" (Page 46)

"If the resolution had been tied to the naval action of the afternoon of 2 August, or to the communist bombing of the officers' quarters in Saigon on Christmas Eve 1964, or even to the VC sapper attack on the air base at Bien Hoa on 1 November 1964, then the administration at least would have had an actual incident upon which to base support for it. Then any reconsideration of the resolution would have centered solely on it and not the incident on which it was based." (Page 47)

References

Glossary

- **A-1H Skyraider:** A type of propeller-driven fighter-bomber used by the U.S. Navy.
- **A-4 Skyhawk:** A type of jet fighter-bomber used by the U.S. Navy.
- **AN/SPG-53:** A type of fire control radar.
- **AN/SPS-40:** A type of long-range air search radar.
- **Bach Dang:** A Vietnamese salvage tug.
- **Bay Chay:** A point near Haiphong harbor.
- **C3I:** Command, Control, Communications, and Intelligence. This term refers to the systems of communication, control, and information gathering that a military force uses in planning and executing its operations.
- **CAP:** Combat air patrol. A combat air patrol is a group of aircraft assigned to patrol an area to protect friendly forces.
- **chong chongs:** The Vietnamese word for a small, single-engine aircraft.
- **CINCPAC:** Commander in Chief, Pacific. This was the command structure for the U.S. Pacific Fleet and its various subcommands, including the Seventh Fleet.
- **Cipher:** A code used to encrypt a message..
- **Colt:** A type of small transport biplane used by North Vietnam.
- **COMINT:** Communications intelligence. Communications intelligence is a subset of signals intelligence and refers specifically to the analysis of communications signals for military purposes.
- **COMUSMACV:** Commander, Military Assistance Command, Vietnam.
- **Constellation:** A U.S. aircraft carrier.
- **Craig:** A U.S. destroyer.
- **Critic-Follow Up:** This is a subsequent message that elaborates on the original Critic.
- **Critic:** This refers to a Critical Message, a type of urgent communication in the U.S. military. Critics are used to inform commanders of potentially dangerous situations that may require immediate action.
- **Danang:** A major port city in South Vietnam.
- **Depth charge:** A type of explosive charge that is used to attack submarines.
- **DIA:** Defense Intelligence Agency
- **DRV:** Democratic Republic of Vietnam. The Democratic Republic of Vietnam was the communist North Vietnamese government, as opposed to the South Vietnamese government.
- **DSU:** Direct Support Unit. A direct support unit is a specialized unit in the military that provides direct support to a larger military unit.
- **ELINT:** Electronic intelligence. Electronic intelligence is another subset of signals intelligence and refers to the analysis of signals from electronic devices that are not intended for communications, such as radars, sonars, and emitters for electronic weapons systems.
- **F-8E Crusader:** A type of jet fighter-bomber used by the U.S. Navy.

- **File time:** The time when a message is entered into a log..
- **Flash precedence:** The highest level of precedence used in U.S. military communications. A flash precedence message must be transmitted immediately and takes priority over all other messages.
- **FOIA:** Freedom of Information Act. The Freedom of Information Act is a U.S. law that allows people to obtain access to records from U.S. government agencies.
- **General Quarters:** A wartime order that puts a ship's crew on high alert.
- **Golf:** Golf time is the time zone used in the Gulf of Tonkin.
- **Haiphong:** A major port city in North Vietnam.
- **Hanoi:** The capital of North Vietnam.
- **Hon Gio:** An island in North Vietnam.
- **Hon Matt Island:** An island in North Vietnam.
- **Hon Me Island:** An island in North Vietnam.
- **Hon Ngu Island:** An island in North Vietnam.
- **Hotel:** Hotel time is the time zone used by the U.S. Navy.
- **JCS:** Joint Chiefs of Staff. The Joint Chiefs of Staff is the command structure for the U.S. military.
- **Linebacker:** A U.S. air campaign against North Vietnam.
- **Luc Luong Dae Biet or Biet Kich:** South Vietnamese Special Forces.
- **MACV:** Military Assistance Command, Vietnam. This was the command structure for U.S. military operations in Vietnam.
- **Maddox:** A U.S. destroyer.
- **Max:** A type of trainer aircraft used by North Vietnam.
- **Morton:** A U.S. destroyer.
- **My Due:** A town in North Vietnam.
- **Nasty:** A type of patrol boat built in Norway.
- **NCA ACC:** National Cryptologic Archives Accession Number
- **NSACSS:** National Security Agency/Central Security Service
- **NSG:** Naval Security Group. The Naval Security Group was the U.S. Navy's cryptologic organization, responsible for signals intelligence in support of naval operations.
- **OPLAN:** Operations Plan. In the military, OPLAN refers to the specific, detailed plans that guide military operations. Each OPLAN will have its own designation.
- **P-4:** A class of patrol torpedo boat supplied by the Soviet Union.
- **PFIAB:** Presidential Foreign Intelligence Advisory Board
- **Phu Bai:** A town near Danang.
- **Port Wallut:** A port in North Vietnam.
- **Precedence:** A classification for the urgency of a military message, such as Flash, Immediate, Priority, and Routine.
- **Quang Khe:** A naval base in North Vietnam.
- **Radford:** A U.S. destroyer.
- **Richard S. Edwards:** A U.S. destroyer.
- **Rolling Thunder:** A U.S. air campaign against North Vietnam.
- **Romeo:** Romeo time is the time zone used in the eastern United States.

- **Saigon:** The capital of South Vietnam.
- **San Miguel:** A naval base in the Philippines.
- **SIGINT:** Signals intelligence. Signals intelligence is a broad term that generally refers to the collection and analysis of electronic signals to obtain military intelligence, but in this context, SIGINT means the analysis of communications signals to learn what the enemy is doing. Signals intelligence in general can involve the analysis of communications signals, non-communications signals such as radar or sonar, or various emissions from weapons systems.
- **Skin Head:** A type of surface search radar.
- **Starshell:** A type of illuminating flare.
- **Studies and Observations Group (SOG):** A U.S. Special Forces unit that conducted covert operations in Southeast Asia.
- **Swatow:** A class of patrol boat supplied by China to North Vietnam.
- **Technical supplement:** An attachment to a report that contains the original text of a message.
- **Thanh Hoa:** A province in North Vietnam.
- **Thong Nhat:** A North Vietnamese merchant ship.
- **Ticonderoga:** A U.S. aircraft carrier.
- **Timberwork:** The codename for maritime operations during OPLAN 34A.
- **Turner Joy:** A U.S. destroyer.
- **VC:** Viet Cong. The Viet Cong was the armed force of the National Liberation Front of South Vietnam, which sought to unify Vietnam under a communist government.
- **Vinh Son:** A port city in North Vietnam.
- **Worksheet:** A written record of the steps taken to decrypt a message.
- **Zulu:** Zulu time is the international standard time, based on Greenwich Mean Time.

Timeline

July 30, 1964: South Vietnamese commandos attack Hon Me Island.

July 31, 1964: South Vietnamese commandos attack Hon Ngu Island near Vinh.

August 1, 1964: A DRV patrol boat, T-146, tracks the Maddox.

August 1, 1964: The DRV naval base at Ben Thuy decides to fight the Maddox.

August 2, 1964: The Maddox is attacked by North Vietnamese torpedo boats.

August 2, 1964: Four jets from the carrier Ticonderoga attack the North Vietnamese boats, leaving one dead in the water and two damaged.

August 2, 1964: The Maddox and Turner Joy are ordered to return to the patrol area.

August 3, 1964: President Johnson announces the Desoto patrols will continue.

August 3, 1964: The State Department protests the attacks on the Maddox.

August 3, 1964: The Maddox and Turner Joy are advised to avoid the area bounded by the 17th and 18th parallels.

August 3, 1964: A four-boat task group, as part of Operation 34A, shells the radar site at Vinh Son.

August 3, 1964: T-142 reports to T-146, for relay to Port Wallut, its after-action report on the events of August 2.

August 4, 1964: The Maddox and Turner Joy begin their patrol.

August 4, 1964: Haiphong informs T-142 that the Maddox is traveling on a southwest heading.

August 4, 1964: The Maddox receives a Critic from Phu Bai stating that a DRV naval operation is planned against the Desoto patrol.

August 4, 1964: The Maddox detects two "skunks" (surface contacts) and three "bogies" (air contacts) on its radar.

August 4, 1964: The Maddox and Turner Joy acquire more radar contacts.

August 4, 1964: The Maddox fires at the radar contacts.

August 4, 1964: The Maddox loses the radar contacts.

August 4, 1964: The Maddox detects another radar contact, only 15 miles to the southwest.

August 4, 1964: The radar return disappears.

August 4, 1964: The Maddox and Turner Joy detect radar contacts closing at nearly 40 knots.

August 4, 1964: Herrick informs CINCPACFLT that he has commenced firing on the attacking PT boat.

August 4, 1964: The return on the Maddox's radar disappears.

August 4, 1964: The return on the Turner Joy's radar disappears.

August 4, 1964: More radar contacts are detected.

August 4, 1964: The Turner Joy fires over 300 rounds.

August 4, 1964: Herrick reports his doubts about the attack.

August 4, 1964: McNamara calls the president with the news of the imminent attack.

August 4, 1964: The flash message from the destroyers that they are under attack reaches the Pentagon.

August 4, 1964: President Johnson approves a retaliatory strike against North Vietnamese naval bases.

August 4, 1964: Admiral Ulysses S. Sharp calls the Pentagon expressing doubts about the reported attack.

August 4, 1964: McNamara meets with the JCS to evaluate the evidence on the attack.

August 4, 1964: NSA releases a translation of a message from T-142 reporting the DRV's losses.

August 4, 1964: The JCS orders an urgent recall of the 34A mission.

August 5, 1964: CINCPAC receives the order to execute the retaliatory raid, code-named Pierce Arrow.

August 5, 1964: Naval strike aircraft from Ticonderoga are launched against North Vietnamese naval installations.

August 5, 1964: A North Vietnamese naval entity reports to an unidentified station a recap of the previous combat with the Americans.

August 6, 1964: DIRNSA queries the NSG detachment aboard the Maddox for intercept information related to the attack.

August 6, 1964: The DSU aboard the Maddox reports it has no manual morse intercept and no voice intercept.

August 6, 1964: NSA issues its first summary report of the 4 August action.

August 8, 1964: San Miguel transmits its second intercept from T-142 to NSA.

September 16, 1964: The USS Morton and the USS Richard S. Edwards begin a Desoto mission.

September 18, 1964: The DRV naval authorities order their ships and posts to be on alert and to be aware for "provocations" by the Americans.

September 18, 1964: A message is passed from an unidentified DRV naval authority ordering all ships to take precautions against possible South Vietnamese maritime commandos.

September 18, 1964: The Morton and Edwards acquire radar contacts.

September 18, 1964: The Morton fires a warning shot at one of the contacts.

September 18, 1964: The Morton and Edwards open fire.

September 18, 1964: The JCS orders a search of the area for debris to confirm the attacks.

September 19, 1964: The JCS continues to request data on the attacks from all the intelligence and combat commands.

September 20, 1964: NSA corrects a Critic by San Miguel which claimed that the DRV was planning to attack the Desoto patrol.

September 20, 1964: The Desoto missions are indefinitely suspended.

October 14, 1964: A chronology of events concerning the 2-5 August Gulf of Tonkin incidents is released.

February 1965: The VC sapper attack on the air base at Bien Hoa occurs.

February 1965: The US initiates the Rolling Thunder air campaign.

February 1968: Secretary of Defense McNamara testifies before the Senate Foreign Relations Committee regarding the incident.

February 1972: Senator Barry Goldwater comments on the incident.

August 1975: The Senate Select Committee on Intelligence approaches NSA about the Gulf of Tonkin incident.

Distribution

Cryptologic Quarterly is published four times a year by the Center for Cryptologic History, NSA. The publication is designed as a working aid and is not subject to receipt, control, or accountability. Distribution is made to branch level; further dissemination is the responsibility of each branch. Extra copies or those for which there is no further need should be returned to the Editor for disposition.

Contributions

Contributions to *Cryptologic Quarterly* should be sent to

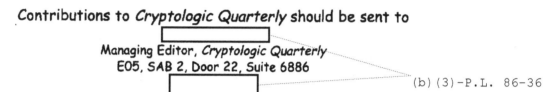

Managing Editor, *Cryptologic Quarterly*
E05, SAB 2, Door 22, Suite 6886

(b)(3)-P.L. 86-36

Electronic submissions can be made via email. Such submissions should include a pdf (portable document format) version, as well as a txt (text) version of the article. Each article should include an abstract. Authors are responsible for determining the classification of submitted articles. If computer disks are submitted, authors must ensure that they are virus-free. All material used in the publication of an article is destroyed when no longer needed unless the author requests that it be returned. *Cryptologic Quarterly* will not accept articles written anonymously or with a pseudonym.

Deadlines for Submissions to the Quarterly

Spring issue	15 February
Summer issue	15 May
Fall issue	15 August
Winter issue	15 November

Reproduction and Dissemination

Contents of any issue of *Cryptologic Quarterly* may not be reproduced or further disseminated outside the National Security Agency without the permission of the NSA/CSS Office of Policy.

(U) Skunks, Bogies, Silent Hounds, and the Flying Fish: The Gulf of Tonkin Mystery, 2-4 August 1964

ROBERT J. HANYOK

(C//SI) The Gulf of Tonkin incidents of 2 to 4 August 1964 have come to loom over the subsequent American engagement in Indochina. The incidents, principally the second one of 4 August, led to the approval of the Gulf of Tonkin Resolution by the U.S. Congress, which handed President Johnson the carte blanche charter he had wanted for future intervention in Southeast Asia. From this point on, the American policy and programs would dominate the course of the Indochina War. At the height of the American involvement, over a half million U.S. soldiers, sailors, airmen, and marines would be stationed there. The war would spread across the border into Cambodia and escalate in Laos. Thailand assumed a greater importance as a base for supporting the military effort, especially for the air war, but also for SIGINT purposes of intercept and direction finding.

(U) At the time, the Gulf of Tonkin incidents of August were not quite so controversial. According to the Johnson administration, the issue of the attacks was pretty much cut and dried. As the administration explained, our ships had been in international waters – anywhere from fifty to eighty miles from the DRV coastline by some calculations, during the alleged second attack – and were attacked twice, even though they were innocent of any bellicose gestures directed at North Vietnam. Secretary of Defense Robert McNamara had assured the Senate that there had been no connection between what the U.S. Navy was doing and any aggressive operations by the South Vietnamese.[1] Washington claimed that the United States had to defend itself and guarantee freedom of navigation on the high seas.

(U) However, within the government, the events of 4 August were never that clear. Even as the last flare fizzled in the dark waters of the South China Sea on that August night, there were conflicting narratives and interpretations of what had happened. James Stockdale, then a navy pilot at the scene, who had "the best seat in the house from which to detect boats," saw nothing. "No boats," he would later write, "no boat wakes, no ricochets off boats, no boat impacts, no torpedo wakes – nothing but black sea and American firepower."[2] The commander of the *Maddox* task force, Captain John J. Herrick, was not entirely certain what had transpired. (Captain Herrick actually was the commander of the destroyer division to which the *Maddox* belonged. For this mission, he was aboard as the on-site commander.) Hours after the incident, he would radio the Commander-in-Chief, Pacific (CINCPAC) telling them that he was doubtful of many aspects of the "attack."

(U) It would be years before any evidence that an attack had not happened finally emerged in the public domain, and even then, most reluctantly. Yet, remarkably, some of the major participants in the events still maintained that the Gulf of Tonkin incident had occurred just as it had been originally reported. Secretary of Defense Robert McNamara, in his memoirs *In Retrospect*, considered the overall evidence for an attack still convincing.[3] The U.S. Navy's history of the Vietnam conflict, written by Edward J. Marolda and Oscar P. Fitzgerald (hereafter referred to as the "Marolda-Fitzgerald history"), reported that the evidence for the second attack, especially from intelligence, including a small amount of SIGINT, was considered conclusive.[4]

Derived From: NSA/CSSM 123-2
             24 February 1998
Declassify On: X1

(U) The public literature on the Gulf of Tonkin for years has been overwhelmingly skeptical about the 4 August battle. Articles that appeared in magazines within a few years illustrated the general inconsistency in the descriptions of the incident of 4 August by simply using the conflicting testimony from the officers and crews of both ships. The first major critical volume was Joseph Goulden's *Truth Is the First Casualty*, published in 1969. The most complete work to date is Edwin Moise's *Tonkin Gulf and the Escalation of the Vietnam War*. Moise's work has the dual advantage of using some Vietnamese sources, as well as small portions of a few SIGINT reports released to the author under a Freedom of Information Act request. Yet, even what few scraps he received from NSA were enough to raise serious questions about the validity of the SIGINT reports cited by the administration which related to the 4 August incident.[5]

(S//SI) The issue of whether the available SIGINT "proved" that there had been a second attack has been argued for years. In 1968, Robert McNamara testified before Senator William Fulbright's Foreign Relations Committee's hearings on the Gulf of Tonkin that the supporting signals intelligence was "unimpeachable." On the other hand, in 1972 the deputy director of NSA, Louis Tordella, was quoted as saying that the 4 August intercepts pertained to the 2 August attacks. In a 1975 article in the NSA magazine *Cryptolog*, the Gulf of Tonkin incident was retold, but the SIGINT for the night of August 4 was not mentioned, except for the "military operations" intercept, and even then without comment.[6] The Navy's history of the Vietnam War would misconstrue the SIGINT (disguised as unsourced "intelligence") associating portions of two critical intercepts and implying a connection in the evidence where none could be established.[7]

(C//SI) Except for the sizable collection of SIGINT material within NSA, and a much smaller amount from the archives of the Naval Security Group (which essentially duplicates portions of the NSA holdings), almost all relevant material relating to the Gulf of Tonkin incidents has been released. Although the questions about what happened in the Gulf of Tonkin on the night of 4 August have been fairly well answered by the evidence from all of the other sources – radar, sonar, eyewitness, and archival – the SIGINT version needs to be told. This is because of the critical role that SIGINT played in defining the second attack in the minds of Johnson administration officials. Without the signals intelligence information, the administration had only the confused and conflicting testimony and evidence of the men and equipment involved in the incident. It is difficult to imagine the 5 August retaliatory air strikes against North Vietnamese naval bases and installations being ordered without the SIGINT "evidence." [8] Therefore, it is necessary to recount in some detail what signals intelligence reported.

(S//SI) For the first time ever, what will be presented in the following narrative is the *complete* SIGINT version of what happened in the Gulf of Tonkin between 2 and 4 August 1964. Until now, the NSA has officially maintained that the second incident of 4 August occurred. This position was established in the initial SIGINT reports of 4 August and sustained through a series of summary reports issued shortly after the crisis. In October 1964, a classified chronology of events for 2 to 4 August in the Gulf of Tonkin was published by NSA which furthered the contention that the second attack had occurred.

(S//SI) In maintaining the official version of the attack, the NSA made use of surprisingly few published SIGINT reports – fifteen in all. The research behind the new version which follows is based on the discovery of an enormous amount of never-before-used SIGINT material. This included *122* relevant SIGINT products, along with watch center notes, oral history interviews, and messages among the various SIGINT and military command centers involved in the Gulf of Tonkin incidents. Naturally, this flood of new information changed dramatically the story of that night of 4/5 August. The most important element is that it is now known what the North Vietnamese Navy was doing that night. And with this information a nearly complete story finally can be told.

(S//SI) Two startling findings emerged from the new research. First, it is not simply that there is a different story as to what happened; it is that *no attack* happened that night. Through a compound of analytic errors and an unwillingness to consider contrary evidence, American SIGINT elements in the region and at NSA HQs reported Hanoi's plans to attack the two ships of the Desoto patrol. Further analytic errors and an obscuring of other information led to publication of more "evidence." In truth, Hanoi's navy was engaged in nothing that night but the salvage of two of the boats damaged on 2 August.

(S//SI) The second finding pertains to the handling of the SIGINT material related to the Gulf of Tonkin by individuals at NSA. Beginning with the period of the crisis in early August, into the days of the immediate aftermath, and continuing into October 1964, SIGINT information was presented in such a manner as to preclude responsible decisionmakers in the Johnson administration from having the complete and objective narrative of events of 4 August 1964. Instead, only SIGINT that supported the claim that the communists had attacked the two destroyers was given to administration officials.

(S//SI) This mishandling of the SIGINT was not done in a manner that can be construed as conspiratorial, that is, with manufactured evidence and collusion at all levels. Rather, the objective of these individuals was to support the Navy's claim that the Desoto patrol had been deliberately attacked by the North Vietnamese. Yet, in order to substantiate that claim, all of the relevant SIGINT could not be provided to the White House and the Defense and intelligence officials. The conclusion that would be drawn from a review of all SIGINT evidence would have been that the North Vietnamese not only did not

attack, but were uncertain as to the location of the ships.

(S//SI) Instead, three things occurred with the SIGINT. First of all, the overwhelming portion of the SIGINT relevant to 4 August was kept out of the post-attack summary reports and the final report written in October 1964. The withheld information constituted nearly 90 percent of all available SIGINT. This information revealed the actual activities of the North Vietnamese on the night of 4 August that included salvage operations of the two torpedo boats damaged on 2 August, and coastal patrols by a small number of DRV craft. As will be demonstrated later in this chapter, the handful of SIGINT reports which suggested that an attack had occurred contained severe analytic errors, unexplained translation changes, and the conjunction of two unrelated messages into one translation. This latter product would become the Johnson administration's main proof of the 4 August attack.

(S//SI) Second, there were instances in which specious supporting SIGINT evidence was inserted into NSA summary reports issued shortly after the Gulf of Tonkin incidents. This SIGINT was not manufactured. Instead, it consisted of fragments of legitimate intercept lifted out of its context and inserted into the summary reports to support the contention of a premeditated North Vietnamese attack on 4 August. The sources of these fragments were not even referenced in the summaries. It took extensive research before the original reports containing these items could be identified.

(S//SI) Finally, there is the unexplained disappearance of vital decrypted Vietnamese text of the translation that was the basis of the administration's most important evidence – the so-called Vietnamese after-action report of late 4 August. The loss of the text is important because the SIGINT record shows that there were critical differences in the English translations of it issued both by the navy intercept site in the Philippines and

NSA. Without the individual texts (there were two of them), it is difficult to determine why there are critical differences in the translations and more importantly, to understand why two separate North Vietnamese messages were combined into one translation by NSA.

(U) Before a discussion can begin, it is necessary to understand how the Gulf of Tonkin incidents came to happen, the way they did, and what their significance was for the Johnson administration. To do that, we need to consider the Desoto mission that the *Maddox* was conducting at the time, as well as the Defense Department's OPLAN-34A missions against the Democratic Republic of Vietnam (DRV). It was the convergence of the two that embroiled that ship in the crisis in the Tonkin Gulf.

(U) The Desoto Missions

(S//SI) Desoto was the covername for a U.S. Navy signals intelligence collection program begun in 1962 in which naval SIGINT direct support units (DSU) were placed on board American destroyer patrols along the Asiatic coastline in the western Pacific

(S//SI) Physically, Desoto mission destroyers were unique in their configuration – a small van lashed to the ship which housed intercept positions for voice and manual morse communications. There also was a position which intercepted noncommunications emissions such as radars, referred to as electronic intelligence or ELINT. Finally, a communications position, which allowed the detachment to send and receive messages from the other monitoring stations in the area, as well as other SIGINT organizations and commands, via the Criticomm communications system, was located in the hut. The hut was manned in shifts from a complement of twelve to eighteen officers and men from the Navy's cryptologic element, known as the Naval Security Group (NSG). However, contrary to some asser-

tions, the Desoto missions were not the functional or operational equivalent of the ubiquitous Soviet electronic collection trawlers.[9] The Desoto missions primarily served the mission needs of local commanders, although they received technical support in the way of technical working aids and intercept data from NSA. (S//SI)

(U) The Desoto patrols had a two-part mission: to collect intelligence in support of the embarked commander and higher level authorities and to assert freedom of navigation in international waters. The early Desoto missions in the waters   had been tracked by the coastal radar surveillance networks belonging to the naval forces   While an occasional communist patrol ship would come out and shadow the U.S. patrol, little else happened.

(U) However, when the Desoto patrol first was proposed for the waters in Southeast Asia, its

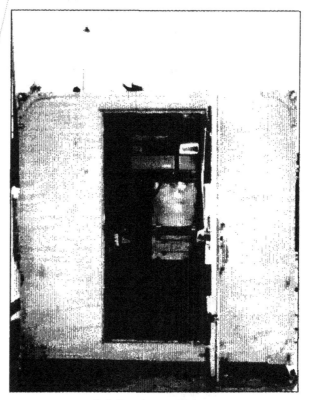

(U) Desoto mission van

mission was expanded. First of all, the commander, Seventh Fleet, wanted the patrol to move in closer than the original twenty-mile limit – as close as twelve miles. Additionally, the Desoto mission was expanded to include a broader collection of "all-source intelligence," namely, photographic, hydrographic, and meteorological information.[10]

(U) In mid-January 1964, COMUSMACV requested that the Desoto patrol scheduled for February (USS *Radford*, DD-446) be designed to provide the forthcoming OPLAN-34A program with critical intelligence regarding North Vietnam's ability to resist its projected commando operations. However, in this case, the *Radford*'s mission was canceled so as to not interfere with OPLAN-34A missions planned for the first two weeks of February.[11]

(U) This is an important point, although a subtle one, for understanding the events of 2 to 4 August. Inasmuch as there was an interworking between the two programs, and this remained a point of contention in later congressional hearings, as well as a source for speculation by the press, the Desoto mission remained merely one of collection of intelligence which could be of use to the OPLAN-34A planners and commanders back in Danang and the Pentagon. There was no direct operational connection between the two programs. They were managed under separate offices and were not known to coordinate mission planning, except for warnings to the Desoto patrol to stay clear of 34A operational areas. At least that was the understanding back in Washington.[12]

(U) In early July, General Westmoreland requested more intelligence on Hanoi's forces which were capable of defending against an expanded OPLAN-34A program. Specifically, Westmoreland required intelligence on the DRV's defenses in those areas targeted for July operation – Hon Me, Hon Nieu, and Hon Matt Islands, as well as the area around the port of Vinh Son,

south of the islands. In response, Admiral Sharp, CINCPAC, issued a new directive for a Desoto patrol whose purpose was "determining DRV coastal patrol activity."[13]

(U) That the two missions might run up physically against one another was a consideration at both MACV in Saigon and CINCPAC (and CINCPACFLT) in Honolulu. But Westmoreland assured the navy commanders that as long as the Desoto patrol stayed within its schedule and area of operations, there would be no problem. Westmoreland added that all the Studies and Observations Group (SOG), which ran the OPLAN-34A missions, needed in the way of an

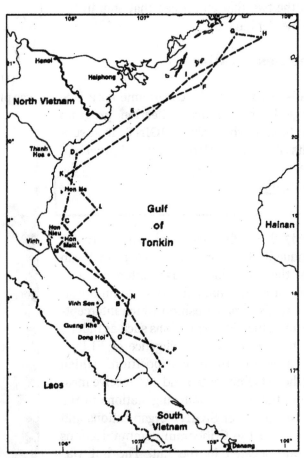

(U) Gulf of Tonkin region of interest to OPLAN-34A and Desoto missions' alphabetic points denote Desoto mission start and stop positions.
(Courtesy of Naval Historical Center)

alert, was thirty-six hours' notice of any change. They could then adjust any planned 34A operation. The navy accepted these reassurances from MACV.[14]

(S//SI) The first Desoto mission in the Tonkin Gulf region ran from February to March 1964. The USS *Craig* (DD-885) sailed near Hainan Island towards the Vietnamese coast and then turned back north towards Macao and Taiwan.

The North Vietnamese tracked the *Craig* as it swung south of Hainan Island, but had made no reaction even though they knew that it was a U.S. warship. It was uncertain to the Americans what the Vietnamese precisely knew of the *Craig* or its mission,

(S//SI) During this mission, there was a Naval Security Group DSU aboard whose task was to provide tactical intelligence to the *Craig's* commander, as well as intercept unique communications and electronic intelligence in reaction to the vessel's presence. The *Craig* also received support from the SIGINT facilities in the region: the navy and air force COMINT sites in the Philippines

No Vietnam-based sites were involved since the area of *Craig's* mission barely touched on the DRV's territorial waters, and then only briefly, although it was suspected that the North Vietnamese navy at least once did report the *Craig's* position.[17]

(U) However, there were two critical differences between the *Craig's* Desoto mission and that of the *Maddox* which followed it in late July and August: The *Maddox* would sail along the entire DRV coastline, while, at the same time, OPLAN-34A maritime missions against North Vietnamese coastal installations were being carried out. By July, the North Vietnamese were reacting aggressively to these raids, pursuing and attacking the seaborne commando units.

(TS//SI) In mid-July 1964, the JCS approved another Desoto mission, which would concentrate on collecting intelligence on North Vietnam's coastal defense posture. The USS *Maddox*, under the command of Captain John Herrick, loaded up its intercept van in the [   ] The sixteen members of the DSU boarded, and the ship departed for the Gulf of Tonkin. The *Maddox* had received no additional instructions to its standard collection mission and apparently was not aware of specific OPLAN 34A missions in the area.[18] However, the *Maddox* was not on a purely passive mission. U.S. intercept sites in the area were alerted to the real reason for the Desoto missions, which was to *stimulate and record* (my italics) North Vietnamese [   ] reactions in support of the U.S. SIGINT effort.[19]

(TS//SI) CINCPAC's orders to Herrick were equally explicit and ambitious: locate and identify all coastal radar transmitters, note all navigational aids along the DRV's coastline, and monitor the Vietnamese junk fleet for a possible connection to DRV/Viet Cong maritime supply and infiltration routes.[20] Whether these missions could be completed was questionable: the DSU was limited by its few positions and equipment in collecting such a large amount of communications. The *Maddox* had been ordered by CINC-PAC to stay eight nautical miles from the North Vietnamese coastline, but only four miles from

(U) USS *Maddox* (DD 731), in August 1964

(U) Captain John J. Herrick (left), the on-site task force commander, and Commander Herbert Ogier, commanding officer of the *Maddox*

any of its islands.[21] It would be attacks on these islands, especially Hon Me, by South Vietnamese commandos, along with the proximity of the *Maddox*, that would set off the confrontation.

(U) Operations Plan 34A

(S//SI)

(b)(1)
(b)(3)

(b)(1)
(b)(3)

per CIA

(TS//SI) At the beginning of 1964, the Department of Defense, which had started its own program, assumed control of all of these covert missions. It merged its own project ▢ ▢ and organized all of the new missions under OPLAN 34A-64,

▢ OPLAN 34A originally was planned to last twelve months and was to be a program of selective intrusions and attacks of graduated intensity. The purpose of these actions was to "convince the Democratic Republic of Vietnam leadership that their continued direction and support of insurgent activities in the RVN and Laos should cease." [24]

(TS//SI) The OPLAN reflected the current American strategy of escalation of the war through graduated response. The U.S. established four levels of actions; each proceeding one was a qualitative and quantitative increase in the sensitivity of target selection and the intensity of the application of force. It began with *harassment* attacks and operations, whose cumulative effect, though labeled "unspectacular," was to make Hanoi aware of them to the extent it would allocate forces to counter them. [25] If this approach failed, then the next level – tagged as *attritional* – was to attack important military and civil installations whose loss could cause "temporary immobilization of important resources" which, in turn, might create or increase opposition amongst the North Vietnamese population to the government in Hanoi. The third level, termed *punitive* by the 34A planners, was meant to cause damage, displacement, or destruction of those facilities or installations considered critical to the DRV economy, industry, or security. To protect itself from further attacks would mean that the DRV would have to redeploy resources originally meant to support the war in the south to the

needs of internal security. The planners admitted that the operations at this level would involve large enough forces that they would be necessarily overt. But the planners felt that these attacks could be attributable to the South Vietnamese. [26]

(TS//SI) The final step of the plan was the initiation of an aerial bombing campaign designed to damage the DRV's capacity to support the southern insurrection or cripple its economy to such an extent that it would realize the extent of its losses was not worth the support of the war in the South. At this point, the planners in Washington believed that Hanoi's reaction to the attacks would be based on two factors: its willingness to accept critical damage to its own economy by continuing supporting the war in the South, and the possible support of the People's Republic of China. The plan did suggest that the communists would choose to continue to support the southern front, and it left open the possibility of further operations to offset the anticipated Chinese aid. [27]

(TS//SI) The major operational components of OPLAN 34A were airborne operations that inserted intelligence and commando teams into North Vietnam, and maritime operations (MAROPS) which consisted of hit-and-run raids on coastal installations and facilities. These latter missions were known under the operational title Timberwork. The teams were made up of mostly South Vietnamese Special Forces, known as *Luc Luong Dac Biet* or *Biet Kich*, with some foreign mercenaries (mostly Chinese and Koreans) to crew the attack craft. The American involvement, though extensive in the planning, training, and logistics portions, was minimized to achieve the usual "nonattribution" status in case the raids were publicized by the North. No Americans were allowed to participate in the actual raids.

(U) Despite all of the planning, there was little confidence in the effectiveness of the OPLAN 34A operations. CIA chief John McCone suggested that they "will not seriously affect the DRV or

(U) Norwegian-built "Nasty" fast patrol boat, the primary platform for maritime operations under OPLAN 34A

cause them to change their policies."[28] Defense Secretary McNamara, when he returned from an inspection trip to South Vietnam in March 1964, described OPLAN 34A as "a program so limited that it is unlikely to have any significant effect." The operations were described by other officials as "pinpricks" and "pretty small potatoes."[29]

(U) The Johnson administration was dissatisfied with the initial results of OPLAN 34A and sought a stronger approach. By June 1964, a new OPLAN, designated 37-64, had been developed jointly by the National Security Council, the JCS, and MACV. This new OPLAN called for a three-pronged approach to "eliminate to negligible proportions DRV support of VC insurgency in the Republic of Vietnam." Three military options were put forward: ground action in Cambodia and Laos to eliminate VC sanctuaries and supply points, increased levels of 34A attacks on Hanoi's coastal installations, and South Vietnamese and United States bombing of ninety-eight "preselected" targets in North Vietnam.[30]

(U) If the commando raids had been such failures, why did they continue to be staged? The truth is, Washington was anxious to support the shaky regime of General Khanh, who had succeeded to the presidency of South Vietnam after Diem's assassination. Until a better plan, such as 37-64, could be implemented, then doing "some-

thing," even as ineffective as the raids, was the course Washington chose to follow. In spite of Hanoi's gains for the first six months of 1964, if America's determination to succeed could be communicated to Khanh, then the South Vietnamese might be reassured of the prospects for victory.[31] This was Washington's policy: to prop up Saigon. Yet, this was a structure built on unsupported assertions.

(TS//SI) The reality for Washington was that the increased tempo of maritime commando raids had only raised Hanoi's determination to meet them head on. Through June and July 1964, NSA and the navy monitoring site in the Philippines reported that the conflict along the coast of North Vietnam was heating up. Communications about small boat actions, commando landings, and high-speed chases out at sea were intercepted and reported back to Washington. What the reports showed was a North Vietnamese navy emboldened to more aggressive reactions to incursions by the commandos from the south. For example, on 28 July, after an attack on the island of Hon Gio, DRV *Swatow*-class patrol boats pursued the enemy for *forty-five* nautical miles before giving up the chase.[32] Earlier, on 30 June, another patrol boat had taken potshots at two jet aircraft flying along the coast and claimed a hit.[33]

(S//SI) By early June, Hanoi's stepped-up defensive posture had registered in its radio traffic. On 8 June, NSA reported that the level of North Vietnamese tactical radio communications had increased almost fourfold during the early part of June from the previous period in May, probably in reaction to attacks along its coast. It also reported that DRV naval patrols now seemed to cover its entire coastline.[34] Clearly, Hanoi was determined to defend itself resolutely. Whether or not the Vietnamese believed that the Americans were preparing for a larger war was not important. What was critical was that the situation along North Vietnam's territorial waters had reached a near boil.[35]

(TS//SI) The SIGINT support to OPLAN 34A started at almost the same time as the operations began. Codenamed Kit Kat, the effort required that the then current ceiling of 660 cryptologic personnel in South Vietnam had to be raised. In February 1964, an increase of 130 personnel for Kit Kat was approved by CINCPAC.[36] The ASA moved personnel from the Philippines to Phu Bai, and the Naval Security Group added coverage of North Vietnamese naval communications to its mission at San Miguel in the Philippines. The Air Force Security Service units at Monkey Mountain near Danang increased their coverage of the communications of DRV navy and coastal surveillance posts. A small special SIGINT unit at Tan Son Nhut Airbase, known as the Special Support Group (SSG), was formed in late February to coordinate Kit Kat support between the intercept sites and the Studies and Observations Group.

(S//SI) A few last notes before we review the attacks. It will be necessary to limit the discussion to the role SIGINT played during the incident. Other evidential sources, such as that from the American ships' own radar, sonar, and visual sightings, will be mentioned in passing simply because they are part of the story and cannot be altogether ignored. However, the brunt of the following discussion will center on the SIGINT evidence because of its critical role in *convincing* the

Johnson administration that the attack actually occurred.

(S//SI) Besides the NSG detachment aboard the *Maddox* (USN-467N), other SIGINT elements that were involved in the events of the next three days included a Marine SIGINT detachment (USN-414T), collocated with the Army Security Agency intercept site at Phu Bai (USM-626J), and the NSG site at San Miguel, Philippines (USN-27), which also had a Marine SIGINT contingent, but the latter was not designated separately as was the Marine group at Phu Bai. It would be the intercept and reporting by the Marine unit at Phu Bai and the navy site in the Philippines which would prove critical to the events in the Gulf of Tonkin.

(S//SI)

(S//SI)

(S//SI) A large number of the reports by the various field sites and NSA were issued contemporaneously with the events themselves. A few of these would be cited in the various after-action analyses and postmortems that attended the Gulf of Tonkin. However, many more field translations and reports based on the intercept during the period of the incidents would be issued as late as two to four days after the crisis. The reason for the apparent delay was that the request from NSA for ALL intercept came only on 7 August.[38]

(C//SI) Because of the nature and enormous amount of the SIGINT evidence used here for the very first time in discussing the Gulf of Tonkin crisis, we will need to present it in a format which will highlight that information. Rather than try to retell the story all at once and incorporate the new evidence into the narrative, which could be overwhelming, especially to those readers not intimately familiar with the events of 4 August, a different tack will be used. We will break down the events into their separate days. First, we will review the details of the known engagement of the afternoon of 2 August. While there is no controversy surrounding this fight – at least there is no question that it occurred – there is an important point to draw from it: that is, the North Vietnamese communications profile during a naval combat engagement was revealed. For ease of reference, we shall refer to this communications profile as the "command and control communications and intelligence" system or C3I. This is a functional description used widely in the intelligence and defense communities to describe the process whereby the individual elements of intelligence (information/ intelligence), command and control (interaction by command authorities), and communications (communications links among all operating elements and units) are combined in military operations.

(U) After looking at the "uneventful" day of 3 August, we will consider the "official" version of the engagement of 4 August. Although, as we progress through the narrative, we will consider the problems with the various other pieces of evidence which support the contention that an attack occurred, the emphasis will be on the SIGINT "clinchers," that is, those reports that convinced the Johnson administration that an attack had occurred. These items will be presented when and how they appeared to the participants.

(U) Finally, we will go back over the clinching SIGINT "evidence" of 4 August and illustrate what problems exist with the individual pieces. In this section, the entire scenario of what was reported and, more importantly, what was *not reported*, will be considered. We will review closely the technical problems with the two critical SIGINT reports which prop up all of the other evidence of an attack by the North Vietnamese. In this approach we will consider how the product was developed and the serious problems in translation, composition, and reporting of the information.

(C//SI) One last item. For purposes of clarity, all time references will be marked either Zulu time ("Z," or Greenwich Mean Time) or Golf ("G," or Zulu +7), which is the time zone for the Gulf of Tonkin. While the actual time of the incidents was in local, or Golf time, SIGINT reports were issued in Zulu time. This is done because of the worldwide nature of SIGINT reporting. The use of Zulu time allows for a consistent and universal benchmark for analysts and recipients of the intelligence. To further confuse the issue, the U.S. Navy used Hotel time (Zulu +8) in all of its messages, which is carried over into its history of the Vietnam War. Then there are the events in Washington, D.C., and NSA HQ, Fort Meade, MD, which are in the Eastern time zone, or

(b)(1)
(b)(3)-50 USC 403
(b)(3)-18 USC 798
(b)(3)-P.L. 86-36

Romeo ("R," or Zulu-5 hours). The latter times will be notated "EST" for Eastern Standard Time. All times will be in given in the military twenty-four-hour clock. So, all "P.M." times after 1200 hours can be determined by subtracting 1200 from the time: e.g., 1700 hours equals 5:00 P.M. Also, it must be remembered that events in the Gulf of Tonkin occurred west of the international date line, so that certain events in the region were occurring the next day in terms of Washington's time. For example, if something happened at 1500 hours Zulu, it is reflected as 2200 hours Golf, 2300 hours Hotel and 1000 hours Romeo of the same day. However, a two-hour advance in Zulu time, that is, 1700 hours on 4 August, means 0000 hours Golf and 0100 hours Hotel time on 5 August, while Washington will be 1200 hours on 4 August. For ease of reference, the reader can observe that there is a twelve-hour difference between Washington and the Gulf of Tonkin.

(U) Round One: The 2 August Battle

(S//SI) It all began with the fireworks of the night of 30/31 July 1964, when South Vietnamese commandos struck at Hon Me Island (19°21'N, 105°56'E), located off the central coast of North Vietnam. At first the commandos tried to land and attack a radar station, but were driven off. The raiders then stood offshore in their boats and peppered the installation with machine gun and small cannon fire. At the same time, two other commando boats bombarded Hon Ngu Island (18°48'N, 105°47'E) near the port of Vinh. During the attack, the *Maddox* had drawn off from the scene as required by its orders to stay well out at sea during the night. On the morning of 31 July, as the *Maddox* made for its patrol station near the coast, Captain Herrick observed the retreating commando boats (called "Nasties" after the manufacturer of their boat, "Nast")

heading south. Communist communications were intercepted by the navy monitoring site in the Philippines, which reported the vain attempts by their patrol craft to catch the "enemy." [39]

(S//SI) On the morning of 1 August, the ASA site at Phu Bai, Republic of Vietnam, monitored a DRV patrol boat, T-146, a *Swatow*-class patrol craft communicating tracking data on the *Maddox* to another *Swatow*. At the time, between 0700G to 0730G (0030Z), the *Maddox* was located nine miles southeast of Hon Me Island moving northeasterly. The *Swatow*-class patrol craft was one of a group supplied by the People's Republic of China. It was a fairly large patrol craft displacing sixty-seven tons. It had a top speed of forty-four knots and a cruising speed of twenty knots. It was armed with two 37-millimeter (mm) antiaircraft (AA) gun mounts, two 20-mm AA mounts, and carried up to eight depth charges. This armament limited the *Swatow*'s role to countering other small vessels. The *Swatow* carried the Skin Head surface search radar. The *Swatow*s often worked in tandem with P-4 torpedo boats, acting as communications relays between North Vietnamese naval command centers and the P-4s, whose long-distance communications capability was limited. This was a role that the *Swatow*s filled all during the next few days' action. [40]

(U) *Swatow*-class patrol boat

(S//SI) The T-146 patrol craft also ordered the other craft to turn on its "equipment," which probably referred to its Skin Head radar. However, the *Maddox* did not intercept any emissions from the *Swatow*'s radar. The North Vietnamese boats referred to the track as the "enemy"; the equation of the term to the *Maddox* was made by Phu Bai.[41]

(S//SI) Shortly after 2300G (1600Z) on 1 August, the naval intercept site in the Philippines reported that the DRV naval base at Ben Thuy (18°39′N, 105°42′E) had informed an unidentified entity, possibly the T-146 patrol boat, that it had been "DECIDED TO FIGHT THE ENEMY TONIGHT [1 Group unreadable] WHEN YOU RECEIVE DIRECTING ORDERS." The base also queried the boat if it had received the "enemy's" position change from another naval entity, possibly an authority on Hon Matt Island (18°48′N, 105°56′E).[42] The *Maddox* was informed of this intercept. A half hour after receiving the most recent report, Captain Herrick informed Seventh Fleet and CINCPAC that he had terminated the Desoto mission because of indications of an imminent attack and was now heading east out of the patrol area at ten knots. These indications of an attack were from Vietnamese communications intercepted by the two field sites, as well as the NSG detachment aboard the *Maddox*. Throughout the rest of the day, these stations would monitor the North Vietnamese ship-to-ship and ship-to-shore manual morse and voice communications nets. They intercepted the all-important vectoring information, the orders from shore commands, and all the tactical communications. However, the DRV boats made no hostile moves against the *Maddox* that day.

(S//SI) Throughout the night of 1/2 August, according to the intercepted communist messages, the North Vietnamese continued to track the destroyer as it remained east of Hon Me Island, some twenty-five miles offshore. Still, nothing had happened that night, and so the *Maddox* returned to its patrol line off the DRV coast on 2 August.

(S//SI) During the early morning, the *Maddox*, which was heading along the northern track of its patrol area, was notified of further North Vietnamese tracking of its movements. The North Vietnamese naval motor torpedo boat squadron stationed at Port Wallut command was receiving the tracking. A coastal surveillance radar station on Hon Me may have been ordered to begin tracking the destroyer "continuously." (It is possible that this station had been inactive during the previous day so as to deny any information on its operation parameters from the American monitoring effort.)[43]

(TS//SI) More ominously for the *Maddox*, the communists also had ordered P-4 patrol torpedo boats (MTB) and *Swatow*-class patrol boats to begin concentrating near Hon Me Island later in the morning.[44] These patrol torpedo boats had been supplied by the Soviet Union. The P-4 boat displaced twenty-five tons. Its top speed was fifty knots; its cruising speed was thirty knots. It had two twin 12.7-mm machine-gun mounts and two eighteen-inch torpedo tubes. The P-4 boat also carried a Skin Head surface search radar. The reporting from the American intercept sites construed the Vietnamese boat concentration near Hon Me as a prelude to an attack on the *Maddox*.[45]

(S//SI) NSA feared that an attack on the *Maddox* was in the offing. At 1002G (0302Z) on 2 August, NSA sent an urgent message to a number of commands and sites in the region warning of a possible attack. Included in this message was CINCPACFLT, MACV, and the Commander, 7th Fleet. Ironically, the *Maddox* was not on distribution for this message; the DSU would have received the message, but it was not addressed either. The gist of the message was simple: repeated attacks by "enemy vessels" on Hon Me Island had led Hanoi to make preparations to repel any further assaults. NSA added that

TOP SECRET//COMINT//X1

(U) P-4 motor torpedo boat

"...THE INDICATED SENSITIVITY ON PART OF DRV AS WELL AS THEIR INDICATED PREPARATION TO COUNTER, POS[SI]BLE THE DRV REACTION TO DESOTO PATROL MIGHT BE MORE SEVERE THAN WOULD BE OTHERWISE BE ANTICIPATED." The problem with the *Maddox* not receiving these critical warnings would not be resolved until after the first attack.[46]

(TS//SI) Shortly before noon, at 1144G (0444Z), the Marine SIGINT group attached to the ASA site at Phu Bai, RVN, intercepted a message from the T-142 *Swatow*-class patrol boat to the DRV naval base at Port Wallut which stated that "[WE] HAVE RECEIVED THE ORDERS. [T]146 AND [T]142 DID USE [1 Group unreadable] HIGH SPEED TO GET TOGETHER [PARALLEL] WITH ENEMY FOLLOWING LAUNCHED TORPEDOES."[47] The Phu Bai station issued a Critic, short for a critical message, that alerted all relevant commands, and the *Maddox*, of the planned attack. In the same report, the Phu Bai site added that four boats, T-142, T-146, T-166, and T-135, had been engaged in tracking and following an "enemy" which "is probably the current Desoto mission." The final paragraph of the message added that the DRV naval facility in Port Wallut was acting as the shore-based "coordinator/director" for the surveillance of the probable Desoto vessel.[48]

(S//SI) About a half hour later, at 1218G (0518Z), another Marine SIGINT detachment stationed with the navy monitoring station at San Miguel, Philippines, intercepted the same message. This later intercept is not unusual; it meant that the Vietnamese were retransmitting the message to ensure its reception. However, this intercept was reported in a different manner than Phu Bai's version. The second version was reported as a translation instead of a report. In essence, this meant that the actual intercept was reported, and not a restatement of its contents. Therefore, some interesting items of intelligence, which were missing from the first report, were included.

(S//SI) First of all, the second version contained what is known as the "file time" of the DRV message, that is, the time when the message was entered into a log prior to its transmission by the Vietnamese radio operator on the T-142. In this case, a file time of 1113G was noted. This time reference tells us that there was a half-hour delay between the receipt of the message from the originator and the initial transmittal of the "attack" message (1144G/0444Z), as well as an hour's difference in the second intercept (1218G/0518Z). The differences are interesting for two reasons. First of all, if the intercept times from both American sites reflect the beginning of the actual intercept of the Vietnamese transmission, then the half-hour difference suggests that the "attack" message was sent more than once. Why more

TOP SECRET//COMINT//X1

than once? It is possible that Port Wallut had not received the first transmission from T-142, although the reports from both Marine sites imply that the message was received each time. Secondly, the lag between the file time and the actual transmission time by the Vietnamese, if figured from the American time of intercept, suggests that the Vietnamese were having difficulties in transmitting messages in a timely manner. This delay, as we shall see, becomes an important element in determining the DRV intentions.

(U) At about this time, the three torpedo boats had arrived at Hon Me Island. The *Maddox*, which was steaming on a northeast heading away from the island, had observed visually the arrival of the three boats. Shortly afterwards, the two *Swatow*s were seen by the *Maddox* in the area of Hon Me. The five North Vietnamese boats now were concentrated at the island.

(S//SI) The "attack" message was followed up by another message, this time from Port Wallut to T-146, which was intercepted at 1306G (0612Z) by the Marines in the Philippines. The message instructed T-146 (and probably T-142) to "LEAVE 135 AND TURN BACK TO [THE PATH] OF THE ENEMY." The "135" that T-146 was told to leave turns out not to have been an individual boat, as earlier reported by the Marines, but the squadron designator for the three P-4 torpedo boats which would take part in the upcoming attack. These three boats made up the Section 3 of Squadron 135.

(S//SI) The five boats, which included the P-4 boats, T-333, T-336, and T-339, departed Hon Me Island at about 1300G, quite possibly on their way to seek out the *Maddox*.[49] Within the next hour a set of apparently conflicting orders was sent to the Vietnamese boats. At 1409G (0709Z), Port Wallut notified both *Swatow* craft that the "enemy" was a large ship bearing 125 degrees (from My Duc?) at a distance of nineteen miles at a speed of eleven knots on a heading of twenty-seven degrees. This put the target on a north-by-

northeast heading, which matched that of the *Maddox*. The same message also included a garbled phrase to "THEN DETERMINE," but it is unclear what this phrase meant.[50] However, according to Edwin Moise, the North Vietnamese said that Section 3 received its order to attack the destroyer at 1350G.[51] Since the file time of the message from Port Wallut was 1400G, this may have been the "attack" message.

(S//SI) However, there is a complicating factor. At 1403G (0703Z), just *six minutes earlier*, the site at San Miguel had copied a message from Haiphong to the two *Swatow* patrol boats which told them to "ORDER 135 NOT TO MAKE WAR BY DAY." Furthermore, the message added that all of the boats were ordered to head towards shore (though an intercept of the same transmission by the Marines at Phu Bai ordered the boats first to *pretend* to head towards shore), and then return to Hon Me Island.[52] Although this message was sent shortly after 1400G (0700Z), it contains a file time of 1203G (0503Z). This means that this message, which constitutes an order to recall the boats, was originated some two hours before the order to attack was transmitted! A second intercept of the same message added that T-146 was supposed to order the recall of Squadron 135's torpedo boats.[53] According to Moise, the North Vietnamese claimed that a recall order was sent after the attack message, but T-146 never relayed it in time.[54]

(S//SI) This conflict in orders by command elements from Port Wallut and Haiphong indicates that there was a loss of control of the situation. It further suggests that the DRV naval authority in Haiphong had never wanted the attack to occur, at least not during the day, when conditions were not favorable for surprising the *Maddox*. Since the boats continued their attack on the destroyer, it appears that the recall order was ignored. The deciding factor for the Vietnamese boat commander may have been the much earlier file time of the recall order; the attack message with the more current file time probably superseded everything else in his decision.

(S//SI) At around 1400G, the *Maddox*'s radar detected the approach from the southwest of the three P-4 torpedo boats. Forewarned by the SIGINT of the Vietnamese intentions to attack, the *Maddox* then started turning eastward, then to the southeast and increased its speed from eleven to twenty-five knots. The North Vietnamese boats initially may have missed the turn to the southeast by the *Maddox*. They probably had been visually tracking the American vessel.[55] There is no SIGINT evidence that their Skin Head radars were active, though the Vietnamese claimed the boats used it. Pictures from the action appear to show the radar masts still upright and not lowered in a combat position. By the time the Vietnamese did react to the *Maddox*'s change in course, they found themselves in an unfavorable attack position. They were chasing the *Maddox* from its rear starboard, that is, from the northwest, which meant it would take some time, even with a near twenty-knot advantage in speed, to achieve an optimal firing position for their torpedo run – perhaps as long as thirty minutes before they could execute a turn on an attack heading.

By 1430G, Commander Ogier ordered the *Maddox* to go to general quarters.

(U) At about 1440G (0740Z) the *Maddox* sent a flash precedence message to various commands in the Pacific that she was being approached by high-speed craft with the intention of attacking with torpedoes. Herrick announced that he would fire if necessary in self-defense.[56] He also requested air cover from the carrier *Ticonderoga*, which was then 280 miles to the southeast. Four F-8E Crusaders from the carrier, already aloft, were vectored to the *Maddox*. The destroyer *Turner Joy* (DD-951) was ordered to make best speed to the *Maddox*.

(U) For the next twenty minutes, the chase continued. The Vietnamese boats inexorably closed the gap between themselves and the destroyer. At 1500G, Captain Herrick ordered Ogier's gun crews to open fire if the boats approached within ten thousand yards. At about 1505G, the *Maddox* fired three rounds to warn off the communist boats. This initial action was never reported by the Johnson administration, which insisted that the Vietnamese boats fired first.

(U) USS *Ticonderoga*

(U) A few minutes later the *Maddox* resumed fire. Through the shellfire, the DRV boats bore in on the *Maddox*. But their attacks were ineffective. Within fifteen minutes of *Maddox*'s first salvo, jets from the carrier *Ticonderoga* had arrived and attacked the Vietnamese boats, leaving one dead in the water and the other two damaged. As for the *Maddox*, she was unscathed except for a single bullet hole from a Vietnamese machine gun round.

(U) There would continue to be confusion over losses for some time. The DRV claimed that two aircraft had been shot down. In reality, one of the navy's jets had sustained wing damage during its maneuvering for the attack and was escorted out of the area by another jet. Both aircraft departed the area under full power, the black exhausts trailing from their engines probably appeared as battle damage to the Vietnamese sailors.[57] The damaged navy jet would be forced to land at Danang.

(U) As for the attacking communist vessels, eventually all three struggled back to their bases. The one craft, T-339, thought to be dead in the water and claimed to have been sunk by the Americans, and, incidentally, initially reported sunk by the Vietnamese as well, actually restarted its engines and managed to limp back to shore. On board were four dead and six wounded Vietnamese sailors out of a crew complement of twelve. However, the other Vietnamese boats were unaware of what had happened and reported T-339 as sunk, and would continue to do so for days afterwards.[58]

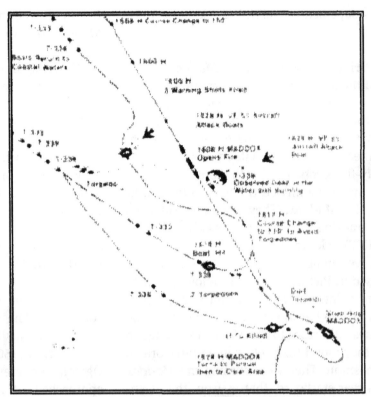

(U) 2 August naval action. Note the use of Hotel time (Z+8/G+1). (Courtesy of Naval Historical Center)

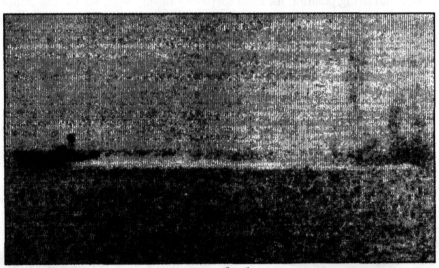

(U) P-4 torpedo boat under fire from *Maddox*, 2 August

(S//SI) At 1630G (2330Z), the Vietnamese patrol boat, T-142, received orders to concentrate back at a location north of Hon Me Island, and to make contact with another possible *Swatow*-class patrol boat, T-165. T-146 also received orders from Haiphong to send two boats out and help the P-4s of Squadron 135 to return.[59] Two days later, on the afternoon of 4 August, T-146 would report to Haiphong the damage to the boats during the attack. T-333 had been hit three times and suffered scattered damage to its water pipes and lifeboat. Its auxiliary engine had been hit and oil pressure was low, suggesting a leak. Still, the boat was assessed as being "lightly damaged." On the other hand, T-336 was described as being "heavily damaged with many holes." Its fuel oil was contaminated, possibly by sea water, and the barrel of one of its deck guns was ruined.[60] The boat's crew had suffered at least two wounded as well. The status of both boats and T-333's crew is important to remember when we look at the events of the later evening of 4 August.

(U) In Washington, the reaction to the attack was relatively subdued. Since no Americans had been hurt, President Johnson wanted the event downplayed while a stern note of protest was sent to the North Vietnamese. (Ironically, this message was the first diplomatic note ever sent to North Vietnam by the United States.) The president had said that we would not "run away"; yet we were not going to "be provocative." However, Hanoi was to be informed in no unambiguous terms that any more unprovoked actions would entail "grave consequences."[61]

(S//SI) The lack of any reprisal was surprising, especially since freedom of navigation was one of the official reasons for the Desoto missions. However, it is likely that there were mitigating factors which caused Washington to pause. Secretary of Defense McNamara was incorrect to claim that the Vietnamese had fired first.[62] At the same time, the Johnson administration had seriously miscalculated the reaction by Hanoi to the OPLAN 34A missions. It had never considered

that the communists might correlate the attacks with the presence of the American destroyer.[63] NSA, monitoring the increasing aggressiveness in DRV naval communications, had seen the possibility and had warned everyone, except the *Maddox*.

(S//SI) Furthermore, Washington, through the intercept of the DRV's naval communications, had seen the confused set of orders sent to the boats, which suggested that Hanoi had lost control of the situation. McNamara would state, "We believed it possible that it had resulted from a miscalculation or an impulsive act of a local commander."[64] It seemed that everyone was trying to defuse the crisis.

(S//SI) DIRNSA, concerned about possible aggressive reactions [ ] ordered all the sites in the region to maintain "extreme collection, processing, and reporting vigilance on part of all with reporting accomplished IAW [in accordance with] established procedures and at precedence appropriate to activity, especially in regards to [ ] reaction."[65] A SIGINT Readiness Level Bravo Lantern was declared. Under this readiness level, eight field sites were tasked by NSA to monitor for any North Vietnamese [ ] reaction to the patrols. The brunt of the intercept and reporting was handed to the navy at San Miguel and the Army and Marine missions at Phu Bai.[66]

(U) The Pentagon was not going to wait around for another incident to happen, either. Plans were put into motion to augment U.S. forces in the region, including deployment of United States Air Force combat aircraft to the Philippines and the dispatch of the carrier *Constellation* to join the *Ticonderoga*. A second destroyer, the *Turner Joy*, already had been dispatched to rendezvous with the *Maddox*. CINCPAC ordered both ships back to the patrol area, seeing it "in our interest that we assert right of freedom of the seas." CINCPACFLT issued new rules of engagement for the next three days which

(U) *USS Turner Joy* (DD-951) in 1964

allowed both ships to approach the North Vietnamese coast as close as eight nautical miles and four miles from its islands. The two destroyers were ordered to arrive at their daylight patrol point about one hour before dawn. One hour before sunset they were ordered to retire east out to sea during the night.[67]

(S) If the Pentagon brass was anxious to insert its ships into harm's way, Captain Herrick was more cautious. In an after-action report transmitted that evening, which reviewed the attack and the successful American defense, he added a warning: the "DRV HAS C[AS]T DOWN THE GAUNTLET AND NO[W] CONSIDERS ITSELF AT WAR WITH US." He added a concern that the DRV's torpedo boats, especially at night, could hide and then approach the destroyers with little warning.[68] He stated that the *Maddox* and the *Turner Joy*, with their five-inch guns and top speed of thirty-three knots, were inadequately armed for defense against such boats. He suggested that the Desoto patrol would be safe only with a cruiser and continuous air cover. One last item was reported by Captain Herrick: the *Maddox*'s long-range, air search radar (AN/SPS-40) was inoperative, and the fire control radar (AN/SPG-53) belonging to the USS *Turner Joy*,

which had just arrived to reinforce him, was out of action indefinitely.[69]

(U) At the close of 2 August, the North Vietnamese boats were hiding in coastal waters caring for their casualties and waiting for orders as to what to do next. The *Maddox* was joined by the *Turner Joy* out at sea, and both were being replenished with ammunition and supplies while under way. They had been ordered to return to the coast at daybreak.

(S//SI) The SIGINT community could be proud of its efforts during the day. The field sites and NSA had intercepted, processed, and reported North Vietnamese naval communications in such a rapid and clear way that everyone in the Pacific command was aware of the approaching attack. It also had provided the information to Washington that suggested that Hanoi's grip on events was less certain than was expected. At the same time, by monitoring the DRV's naval communications, the cryptologists had developed a picture of the command and control elements prior to an attack: extensive tracking by coastal observation posts; the identification of a target and the communication of an attack command; and the use, if limited, of radars in locating the target. The *Maddox* had never been explicitly named as the target of the attack; in fact, there was just the notation of an "enemy"; however, the analysts at Phu Bai, San Miguel, and inside the Desoto hut had correlated the North Vietnamese tracking with the American ship. The *Maddox* had been fixed in the minds of the American cryptologists as an "enemy vessel" to the North Vietnamese; they would be on the lookout for possible new attacks. The question was, though, was Hanoi spoiling for another round with the U.S. Navy?

(U) Interlude: Maneuvers and Watchfulness, 3 August

(U) On 3 August, President Johnson made public the instructions he had issued to the Navy earlier. He said that the patrols would continue in the Gulf of Tonkin, that they would be reinforced by another destroyer with combat aircraft overhead. He added that if attacked in international waters, U.S. forces would attack any force with the intention of not just driving it off, but of "destroying it."

(U) At the same time, the State Department publicized the note it had sent Hanoi protesting the attacks. It concluded with the words "The United States Government expects that the authorities of the regime in North Vietnam will be under no misapprehension as to the grave consequences which would inevitably result from any further unprovoked military action against the United States forces." [70]

(U) Despite the increased North Vietnamese vigilance and the observed sensitivity to American and South Vietnamese naval activity in Hanoi's territorial waters, COMUSMACV went ahead with an OPLAN 34A mission scheduled for the night of 3-4 August. In accordance with an earlier agreement, the Maddox and Turner Joy were advised to avoid sailing in the area bounded by the 17th and 18th parallels. A 34A mission against the radar site at Vinh Son (17°57'N, 106°30'E), which involved a four-boat task group, set sail at 1510G (0810Z) on 3 August. At midnight it shelled the radar station. One of the boats broke off and attacked a nearby security post and was pursued for a short distance by a North Vietnamese patrol craft.

(U) By mid-morning of 3 August the two destroyers were heading to their patrol station, which was about 100 miles northwest of the new

34A mission area. They expected to be on station by early afternoon. However, this location kept them in the area of the island of Hon Me, which was the focus of DRV naval activity during the ensuing day and night.

(S//SI) Meanwhile, the North Vietnamese were concerned with the salvage of their damaged boats. Just past midnight on 3 August, T-142 and T-146 were in the area of Hon Me Island trying to contact another Swatow, T-165, as well as find the missing boats from Squadron 135. At 0300G (2000Z), T-142 sent an after-action report to the T-146 (for relay to Port Wallut), which highlighted the previous afternoon's combat. It included a chronology of the various actions the squadron's boats carried out from 0935G to 1625G when they attacked the Maddox. [71]

(S//SI) Even by mid-afternoon of 3 August, naval headquarters in Haiphong still did not know where the torpedo boats were and demanded that the Swatows inform it when they knew their situation. [72] However, the SIGINT site at Phu Bai misconstrued this search and salvage activity as a prelude to a potentially dangerous concentration of enemy boats. It issued a Critic at 1656G (0956Z), which placed six DRV patrol and torpedo boats near Hon Me Island. [73] However, the report was wrong in that it identified the squadron reference "135" as a boat, as well as locating the two torpedo boats, which, at the time, were still missing. The ominous concentration of boats simply was not occurring. However, this incident revealed how tense the situation had become. It also illustrated a precedent by the field site at Phu Bai for misinterpreting Hanoi's intentions.

(TS//SI) Almost as soon as the two destroyers arrived on station south of Hon Me Island in early afternoon, they were shadowed by a DRV patrol boat which tracked them using its Skin Head radar. [74] The tracking continued through the afternoon into early evening. The Haiphong naval authority and the Swatow boats near Hon Me exchanged position information on the two destroyers as they moved from the north to south and back north on their patrol.[75] At one point, another *Swatow*, T-379, erroneously identified as an SO-1 class subchaser, was ordered to go out and observe "different targets," which probably referred to the American ships.[76] The North Vietnamese also detected aircraft in the area of the Desoto patrol, though it is unclear from their report whose aircraft these were. However, the commander, 7th Fleet, had ordered a continuous combat air patrol accompanying the two destroyers. The navy jets flew their cover to the east of the Desoto position so as to avoid infringing on DRV air space.[77]

(S//SI) By early evening, Haiphong ordered T-142 to track the Desoto patrol. T-379, which earlier had been instructed to observe the Desoto patrol, had sailed to Hon Ngu Island (18°48'N, 105°47'E). It had arrived at 2250G (1550Z) and reported that the situation at sea was "peaceful."[78]

(S) T-142 took up a position to the north of the two destroyers and stayed with them, reporting the location of the American ships to Haiphong either directly to naval HQs or relaying reports through T-146. Both U.S. ships reported being followed from the north at a distance of thirty-eight miles by a DRV patrol craft using its Skin Head radar. By this time, 2252G (1552Z), the Desoto patrol was heading southeast out of the patrol area as had been instructed earlier.[79] Tracking of the destroyers ended soon after when they were out of range.

(S//SI) Meanwhile, the main concern of the DRV navy was the recovery operation for the boats damaged during the 2 August attack. Late in the night of 3 August, Haiphong informed T-142 that the salvage tug *Bach Dang* would soon leave Haiphong (it was not clear from the intercept if the time of departure was 0100G, 4 August/1800Z, 3 August) and head towards Hon Me Island to tow T-333 and T-336 back to

Haiphong or Port Wallut, which was their unit's base.[80] It was expected that the tug would arrive at about noon on 4 August. Meanwhile, T-146 was ordered to stay with the two damaged boats from Squadron 135 and report their position and status.

(U) So ended 3 August. That evening's 34A raid on Vinh Son was protested by Hanoi. In its complaint, it accused the two destroyers of participating in the raid. Although the DRV's own tracking of the two ships had ceased some hours before, and they could not be certain of where the American ships were, the Vietnamese had inferred anyway that the Desoto ships were involved. It may not have been the right conclusion, but the Vietnamese believed it. Washington still did not think that Hanoi would act.

(U) Round 2: "Everything in Doubt"– The 4 August Action

(S//SI) At 0600G (2300Z) on the morning of August 4, the two destroyers turned westward towards the DRV coastline to begin their day's patrol. By 1300G (0600Z) they returned to their duty station off the coast of North Vietnam near Thanh Hoa (20°08'N, 105°30'E), known as point "Delta," where they began to steam to the southwest along the Vietnamese coast. The air cover from the *Ticonderoga* again was overhead and to the east. An hour later, the *Maddox* reported that it had another shadow, this time fifteen miles to the east. The identity of this shadow cannot be determined.

(S//SI) The North Vietnamese had been tracking the Americans. Haiphong informed T-142 at 1610G (0910Z) that they had located the destroyers near 19°36'N and 106°19'E traveling on a southwest heading. However, this last position of the two ships had been acquired by the North Vietnamese some two and one-half hours earlier at 1345G (0645Z).[81] At approximately 1600G (0900Z), following his operational directive from

CINCPAC to be clear of the patrol area by dark, Herrick ordered the patrol to head due east.

(S//SI) At 1115Z (1815G), the naval SIGINT detachment aboard the *Maddox* received a Critic from the Marine SIGINT unit collocated with the ASA at Phu Bai, which stated, "POSS DRV NAVAL OPERATIONS PLANNED AGAINST THE DESOTO PATROL TONITE 04 AUG. AMPLIFYING DATA FOL." [82] Twenty-five minutes later, Phu Bai issued a follow-up report at 1140Z (1840G) which reported, "IMMINENT PLANS OF DRV NAVAL ACTION POSSIBLY AGAINST DESOTO MISSION."[83] The report went on to add that three DRV boats, T-142, T-146, and T-333 had been ordered at 0927Z (1627G), the time the message was intercepted by Phu Bai, to "make ready for military operations the night of 4 August." Although the report did not specify the nature of the military operations, the Marines appear to have concluded that it was an attack against the Desoto. The NSG detachment informed Herrick. Within an hour, at 1240Z, he informed CINCPAC and other commands that he had received "INFO INDICATING ATTACK BY PGN P-4 IMMINENT. MY POSITION 19-10N 107-00E. PROCEEDING SOUTHEAST." [84] At this point, the two ships were about eighty to eighty-five nautical miles from the nearest DRV coastline and began to head southeast at twenty knots.

(S) A short time later, just after 1300Z (2000G), the Desoto vessels acquired their first radar contacts. The *Maddox* reported that it had detected "two skunks" (surface contacts) and three "bogies" (air contacts) on its radars. The surface contacts were about forty to forty-five miles to the *northeast* of the two destroyers, putting them about 100-110 miles away from the Vietnamese coast at sea, but very close to Hainan Island.[85] (The appearance of aircraft returns (bogies) on the destroyer's radar has generally gone unremarked upon by various commentators. Herrick speculated that these were terrain returns. Whatever the case, these false "bogies"

suggest *Maddox*'s air surveillance radar was still malfunctioning.) The *Ticonderoga* ordered the four jets on CAP to cover the two ships. It scrambled four more A1H Skyraiders. Within an hour, the aircraft were overhead.

(S) At about 2045G (1345Z), Herrick reported he had lost the original surface contacts: they had never closed to less than twenty-seven miles from his own ships. At 2108G (1408Z), *Maddox* detected another return – first identified as one boat, later thought to be several boats in a tight formation – this time only fifteen miles away to the southwest, moving towards the destroyers at thirty knots. Nine minutes later, naval A-4 Skyhawks flying air cover were vectored towards the supposed boats. Although the pilots could see the wakes of the destroyers clearly, they could see no boats at the point the radar indicated. At 2131G (1431Z), this radar return disappeared.[86]

(U) Then at 2134G (1434Z) came the most important radar contact of the entire incident. What appeared to be a single boat suddenly appeared on the *Maddox*'s radar screen *east* of the two destroyers at 9,800 yards and closing at nearly 40 knots. The *Turner Joy* detected another object approaching, but on a different heading, distance, and speed. According to Marolda and Fitzgerald, the navy claimed that this was the same return as the *Maddox*'s.[87] At 2137G (1437Z) at a distance of 6,200 yards from the Desoto vessels, the return tracked by the *Maddox* appeared to make a sharp turn to the south. This maneuver was interpreted by the *Maddox* combat information center as a turn after a torpedo run. If this was a torpedo launch, then it was an extraordinarily desperate one. Hanoi's tactical specifications for its P-4s called for torpedo launches at ranges under 1,000 yards. At over 6,000 yards, it was unlikely a torpedo launched at a moving target could hit anything.[88] The sonar operator aboard the *Maddox* detected a noise spike on his equipment, but *did not* report it as a torpedo. This conclusion was reached on the CIC. However, the *Turner Joy* never detected any torpedoes on its sonar. Nor did it detect any torpedoes at all on its sonar that night.[89]

(U) At 2140G (1440Z), Herrick informed CINCPACFLT that he had commenced firing on the attacking PT boat. The *Turner Joy* had begun firing at its return shortly before this. Both destroyers had a difficult time holding a radar lock on their targets. Within five minutes, the return on *Maddox*'s radar, which was moving *away* from the destroyers, disappeared from its screen at a distance of about 9,000 yards. The one that the *Turner Joy* was tracking kept approaching, and at a distance of about 4,000 yards, it disappeared as well.[90]

(U) For the next fifteen minutes all surface contacts were gone from the radars of the two destroyers. Then, at 2201G (1501Z), more contacts were detected coming from the west. Now the thickest part of the naval action commenced. The two destroyers gyrated wildly in the dark waters of the Gulf of Tonkin, the *Turner Joy* firing over 300 rounds madly at swarms of attacking North Vietnamese boats – maybe as many as thirteen – and dodging over two dozen torpedoes.

Another twenty-four star shells had been fired to illuminate the area and four or five depth charges had been dropped to ward off the pursuing boats and the torpedoes. The *Maddox* vectored overhead aircraft to the surface contacts, but time and again the aircraft reached the designated point, dropped flares, and reported they could not find any boats. By the time the attack was considered over at 2335G (1635Z), Herrick reported two enemy patrol boats sunk and another damaged. (The count of the damaged boats varied; Herrick believed that the DRV boats sank one of their own accidentally. It is not understood how he arrived at this conclusion, except as a misinterpretation of the radar data which itself was of dubious quality.)

(U) It should be mentioned again that the radar returns from both ships were not continuous trackings. Rather, they were mostly flashing returns, that is, they appeared on the scope, held for a few sweeps of the radar, then disappeared. Other targets would suddenly appear a few miles from the destroyers, hold for a while and then disappear. They came from all directions. As each return was logged, it was assigned a target designator, a single letter. One officer from the *Turner Joy* described the confusion of proliferating targets this way: "We were getting blotches on the the radar screen – nothing real firm, so we were whacking away at general areas with proximity fuzes, hoping to get something." [91] A target would apparently be hit and then disappear as if it had completely and instantaneously incinerated in an explosion — contrary to what had happened two days earlier when the North Vietnamese PT boats would take several hits but remain afloat afterwards. The *Maddox*'s main gun director

(U) Gulf of Tonkin track, 3-5 August 1964
(Courtesy of the Naval Historical Center)

maintained that the ship was never able to acquire any of the targets during the battle; he figured he was shooting at the high swells brought on by the storms.[92] Ironically, during all of this latter action, the *Maddox* never fired a round; its radar never acquired another target after the initial one detected two hours earlier.[93]

(U) The sonar returns of the supposed torpedo attacks were later determined to be a result of the high-speed maneuvering by both U.S. ships. As we saw above, the first "evidence" of a torpedo launch by the enemy boats came from radar. When one of the radar tracks turned away to the south from a westerly heading, this was interpreted by the Americans as a torpedo launch. The sonar rooms in both destroyers were then alerted to a possible torpedo attack. Four crewmen aboard the *Turner Joy* thought they saw a "white streak" in the water as the ship turned.[94] Both vessels had then gone into wild evasive maneuvers to avoid the torpedoes that were thought to have been launched against them. It was this high-speed gyrating by the American warships through the waters that created all of the additional sonar reports of more torpedoes. Every time one of the destroyers changed course, the sonar reported the distinctive high-speed sounds of torpedoes. Eventually, Herrick and the other officers realized what was happening: the rudders of the two ships had caused the high-speed returns when they reflected the turbulence of the ships' own propellers.[95]

(S) Within an hour of the end of the attack, Herrick relayed his doubts about the attack in an after-action report. After reviewing the number of contacts and possible sinkings, he stated, "ENTIRE ACTION LEAVES MANY DOUBTS EXCEPT FOR APPARENT ATTEMPTED AMBUSH AT BEGINNING."[96] Herrick then suggested in the morning that there be a thorough air reconnaissance of the area for wreckage. In a follow-up message, Herrick added that the *Maddox*

had "NEVER POSITIVELY IDENTIFIED A BOAT AS SUCH."[97]

(U) Herrick's doubts did not sit well with Washington. Since the first Critic warning of the attack, which had arrived at 0740 EST, Washington had been following the action in the Gulf of Tonkin. At 0925 EST, Secretary McNamara had called the president with the news of the imminent attack. At 1000 EST the flash message from the destroyers that they were under attack reached the Pentagon. Within three hours after the attack ended, 1400 EST, President Johnson had already approved a retaliatory strike against North Vietnamese naval bases to be carried out at 1900 EST, 4 August (0700G, 5 August).

(U) Precisely why President Johnson ordered a retaliatory strike so quickly is not totally clear, especially when there was conflicting evidence as to whether it had actually occurred. Johnson was in the midst of a presidential campaign and his opponent, Republican senator Barry Goldwater from Arizona, a noted hawk, would have gained in the race if Johnson had hesitated or refused to retaliate. Johnson, even in his pose as a moderate relative to Goldwater, could hardly appear weak before a public audience demanding a counterstrike.[98] It also has been suggested that when Johnson first learned of the possible attack, that is, the first Critic issued by Phu Bai, he decided to use the warning as an excuse to get Congress to pass what was soon to be known as the Gulf of Tonkin Resolution.[99]

(S) Whatever the president's own rationale for ordering the air strike, he required immediate verification of the North Vietnamese attack because of the doubts that started to be openly expressed within the administration. At around 1400 EST, Admiral Ulysses S. Sharp, CINC-PACFLT, called the Pentagon with the news that "a review of the action makes many reported contacts and torpedoes fired 'appear doubtful' " because of freak weather, over-eager sonar operators, and the absence of visual sightings.[100] McNamara called Sharp, who added that there was "a little doubt on just what exactly went on."[101] Messages buzzed back and forth between Washington and the Pacific, demanding information and then getting contradictory evidence of the attack. The Desoto mission reported that except for possibly the first torpedo report at 2159G (1459Z), all others were caused by reflections off the two destroyers' screws.[102] At the same time, Herrick reported that the air cover from the two carriers was unable to locate the targets because of poor weather. Yet the carrier *Ticonderoga* transmitted its own evaluation in which the pilots had "REPORT[ED] NO VISUAL SIGHTINGS OF ANY VESSELS OR WAKES OTHER THAN TURNER JOY AND M[ADDOX]. WAKES FROM TURNER JOY AND M[ADDOX] VISIBLE FROM 2-3000 YARDS."[103] Crews from the two destroyers reported seeing nothing for certain. One sailor thought he had seen flashes of gunfire, but wasn't sure.

(TS//SI) Then, like a classic *deus ex machina*, along came a second SIGINT report that seemed to clinch the case for an attack. This report was a translation issued by NSA on the 4th of August at 1933Z (1433 EST in Washington) and was leaped upon by administration officials, especially the secretary of defense, Robert McNamara, as direct evidence of the attack. What this translation *appeared* to be was a sort of North Vietnamese after-action report. An unidentified North Vietnamese naval authority had been intercepted reporting that the DRV had "SHOT DOWN TWO PLANES IN THE BATTLE AREA," and that "WE HAD SACRIFICED TWO SHIPS AND ALL THE REST ARE OKAY." It also added that "THE ENEMY SHIP COULD ALSO HAVE BEEN DAMAGED."[104]

(U) At 1640 EST, Admiral Sharp again called McNamara with more information on the attack. Just before 1700 EST, McNamara and the JCS met to evaluate the evidence on the attack. They concluded that it had occurred and that five fac-

tors were critical: "(1) The *Turner Joy* was illuminated [by a searchlight] when fired on by automatic weapons; (2) One of the destroyers observed cockpit [bridge] lights [of one of the DRV patrol boats]; (3) A PGM 142 had shot at two U.S. aircraft (from COMINT); (4) A North Vietnamese announcement that two of its boats were 'sacrificed' (from COMINT); (5) Admiral Sharp's determination that there was indeed an attack."[105]

(U) Of the five pieces of "evidence," two were from the same NSA product issued that afternoon (EST). If the two pieces of visual evidence – the searchlight and cockpit light reports – were contentious, the SIGINT was, in the minds of the secretary of defense, the JCS, and the president, the "smoking gun" evidence needed to justify the air strikes on North Vietnam.[106] So, at 0700G

(U) Burning North Vietnamese patrol boat after 5 August strike

(0000Z) on 5 August, CINCPAC received the order to execute the retaliatory raid, codenamed Pierce Arrow. At 1030G (0330Z), naval strike aircraft from *Ticonderoga* were launched. By early afternoon they hit several targets in the DRV, including almost all of its naval installations.

(U) The Silent Dogs: What the SIGINT Really Did (and Did Not) Report

(S//SI) Events surrounding the apparent second attack had been driven almost exclusively by SIGINT. Herrick's personal doubts, the false sonar readings, the confused radar returns, and the pilots' reports, all subverted the validity of the attack reports. But not the SIGINT. For the Johnson administration, both reports – the initial Critic reporting the North Vietnamese preparations for operations, and the after-action report – acted as factual bookends, propping up the other pieces of contentious evidence. The details of the attack, as contradictory as they were, could be massaged or explained to fit the scenario set by the SIGINT. For example, since there were no reported shootdowns of American aircraft that night, then the North Vietnamese report of downed U.S. planes must have resulted when they had confused illuminating flares for falling aircraft.[107]

(S//SI) However, there were many problems specific to the SIGINT information which emerged almost as soon as it was being reported. In this section we will reconsider what happened that night using all of the relevant SIGINT. We will begin with the initial order to the Vietnamese boats ordering them to make ready for military operations.

(S//SI) **Exhibit A: The First Attack Message**

(S//SI) The first product, the "attack" message, issued at 1115Z (1815G), reported only the fact that there was a possible DRV naval operation planned against the Desoto patrol. At 1140Z

(1840G), this was followed up by a second report from Phu Bai which contained a number of details, such as that T-146 and T-333 were to carry out military operations with T-142. Unlike the messages of 2 August, there was no reference to an "enemy," no tracking to equate to the Desoto patrol, or any indication of the nature of the operations to be carried out by the boats. In fact, the original intercepted message was only the first part of a larger message, the rest of which was not intercepted. So, what might have been in the latter part is unknown, except that it might have amplified the meaning of the type of operation the boats were involved in.

(S//SI) What made this intercept a Critic was the *interpretation* put to it by the Marine SIGINT site at Phu Bai, which stated that this was an "OPERATION PLANNED AGAINST THE DESOTO PATROL." [108] The follow-up report from Phu Bai amplified the original Critic and maintained, as well, that the attack was against the Desoto mission.[109] When one considers the events of 2 August, this interpretation was not totally unfounded; one could see a reference to a military operation being directed against the American warships. However, the text of the intercept never mentioned a target or any objective of the military operation, or even the nature of the operation. As we shall see soon, not everyone who saw this intercept jumped to the same conclusion that an attack against the American ships was being planned.

(S//SI) Another problem is that the decrypted Vietnamese phrase for military operations, *hanh quan*, has an alternate meaning of "forced or long march or movement," which, in a nautical context, could refer to a voyage by both T-146 and T-333. As it turns out, this is the activity that the intercept was actually alluding to.

(S//SI) For at 1440Z, *almost at the precise moment* that Herrick ordered his two destroyers to open fire on the approaching radar returns, the Phu Bai intercept site issued a spot report which

```
Z O 041115Z ZYH

FM USN 414T

TO USN 467N

┌─────────────┐
│             │
└─────────────┘
INFO ┌─────────┐
     └─────────┘
USM 27

NSAPAC REP VIETNAM (C)

DIRNSA

S E C R E T KIMBO

DESOTO

1. POSS DRV NAVAL OPERATION PLANNED AGAINST THE DESOTO PATROL

TONITE 04 AUG. AMPLIFYING DATA FOLS
```

(S//SI) Phu Bai Critic alerting Desoto patrol to possible attack

```
"To 145 & Cadre Khoai. [I U] so that when you have orders the
146 can tow [4 gr M] the 336 back. If the tank truck hasn't yet
come to supply you, then the 146 can transfer fuel to the 333.
With regard to orders, the 333 will carry out military operations
independently with 146. (Continued)
[continuation unavailable]
                                                    4 Aug 0927Z
USN 414T intercepted at 040927Z   Date/time of file: 041558G
```

(S//SI) Translation of the intercepted original of the "attack" order

stated that both DRV torpedo craft, T-336 and T-333, the latter of which earlier had been reported ready to attack the Desoto patrol, were, in fact, being readied *to be towed* to either Haiphong or Port Wallut. This second report carried two salient points: First, at 1946G (1246Z), *Swatow* T-142 reported to Haiphong that the tug *Bach Dang* was unable to return to port. T-142 also included the statement that if the ship [*Bach Dang*] "MET THE DESOTO MISSION, IT WAS TO [A]VOID THEM." [110] Besides being a warning about the Desoto ships, the message also implied that the North Vietnamese thought that the destroyers were close enough to shore to be a threat to DRV vessels, whereas, at this time, the American ships were far out at sea. In all probability, the North Vietnamese had lost track of the American destroyers (an issue which we will discuss further on in this narrative).

(S//SI) The second point of the Phu Bai report was that at 2031G (1331Z) T-142 had informed an authority in Port Wallut that the tug was towing the two craft from Squadron 135. The analysts at Phu Bai added this comment to the end of their report which read, "WITH THE MTB 336 ADDED TO ITS STRING, IT AP[PE]ARS THAT T333 WILL NOT PARTICIPATE IN ANY MILITARY OPERATIONS." So, the boats originally reported being ready to attack the Desoto patrol, were incapable of even moving on their own!

(S//SI) In fact, this attempted salvage of the two damaged torpedo boats would occupy the efforts of Hanoi's sailors for much of the night of 4/5 August. The Vietnamese would try various methods of getting the two damaged P-4s to a port for repairs. During the 2300G hour, T-146 was ordered by Haiphong to escort the *Bach Dang* as it returned to base. When that was completed, T-146 was ordered to Bay Chay, a point near Haiphong harbor.[111] Shortly afterwards, T-142 informed Haiphong that the very busy T-146 was now to tow T-336 back, but since the latter boat was short of fuel, the T-333, which was short of oil but under tow from the *Bach Dang*, could transfer one to five tons of its fuel to its sister vessel.[112] At 1830Z on 4 August (0130G on 5 August), the navy monitoring site at San Miguel intercepted T-142's report to Haiphong that T-146 had completed its preparations for the two torpedo boats by 0100G 5 August (1800Z 4 August).[113] So, in reality, none of the boats named in the original attack Critic in fact participated in anything but salvage efforts.

(S) Remember, Captain Herrick did not know that the original Critic was really an interpretation, and that there was no explicit reference to an attack on his ships. He accepted the Critic's contents as intercept of actual Vietnamese plans to attack his ships when he informed the *Ticonderoga* task group commander of his decision to leave the area. He added his own twist to the report to include specifically the unsupported amplification mentioning the involvement of North Vietnamese P-4 torpedo boats when only one was mentioned as a potential participant in the unidentified operations, and then only if it could be refueled.[114]

(S//SI) The possibility that, even if the interpretation was incorrect, the Marine Critic was justified in light of the events from two days earlier, does not stand up when we consider that another site, the navy intercept station at San Miguel, Philippines, had translated the same "operations order," but reported it in a much different fashion. The navy translated the same intercept and then reported it at a Priority precedence, two levels below a Critic (or one level above Routine). The navy analysts titled the report "REPLENISHMENT OF DRV NAVAL VESSEL." The San Miguel report translated the critical sentence as: "T146 SUPPLY FUEL FOR

THE 333 IN ORDER TO GIVE ORDERS TO PUT INTO OPERATION ((2 GR G)) WITH T146."[115]

(S//SI) The difference (and correctness/incorrectness) between the translations is not important as much as the fact that San Miguel viewed the information as nothing more than the refueling of the damaged torpedo boats. This was in line with an earlier intercept of a query from Haiphong to T-142 asking if T-333 had been refueled yet.[116] Unfortunately, because the San Miguel version was a lower precedence, it was released much later. In fact, it came out at 1838Z (0038G), some two hours after the destroyers had stopped shooting.

(S//SI) The quandary created by the reports about the salvage operations is this: If the original suspect vessels, the two *Swatow*-class patrol and two damaged P-4 torpedo boats, were not participating in the anticipated "attack" against the Desoto patrol, then who exactly was going to attack? No other messages had been intercepted which suggested that any other DRV boats were handed the mission of attacking the American destroyers. In fact, there was no intercept at all which hinted at an attack; nothing at all like what had been intercepted on 2 August. So, if the original culprits were involved in salvage operations, then just what was going on in the Gulf of Tonkin?

(S//SI) For NSA and the rest of the SIGINT participants, the second Phu Bai report should have acted as a brake to any further reporting about an attack. It directly contradicted the interpretation – remember, it was an interpretation only – contained in the initial Critic which claimed an attack was being prepared. At this point, all the SIGINT community could accurately state was that there was no signals intelligence reflecting a planned or ongoing attack against the Desoto mission.

(TS//SI) Except this is not what happened. The second Phu Bai report was not used to report what was going on in the Gulf of Tonkin. Instead, the problem posed by the second Phu Bai report was handled in a curious manner. Late on 4 August, Washington (050130Z August 1964), NSA issued a Gulf of Tonkin situation report which covered the events of 4 to 5 August. At the end of the report, NSA added these interesting sentences: "ALTHOUGH INITIAL MESSAGES INDICATED THAT THE T142, T146, AND T333 WOULD BE INVOLVED IN THE ATTACK . . . SUBSEQUENT MESSAGES [not further identified in the report – a curious lapse by NSA which we will address in detail later] SUGGEST THAT NONE OF THESE [BOATS] WAS INVOLVED. REPORTS FROM THE MADDOX THAT IT WAS UNDER ATTACK SOME SEVENTY NAUTICAL MILES NORTHEAST OF THE NAVAL BASE AT QUANG KHE SUGGEST THAT NAVAL UNITS SUBORDINATE TO THE SOUTHERN FLEET COMMAND . . . WERE INVOLVED. . . ." [117]

(TS//SI) However, the effort to find "culprits" only compounded the errors: the only boats known to be stationed permanently at Quang Khe were Swatow-class patrol boats which did not carry torpedoes.[118] All P-4 torpedo boats staged from Port Wallut far northwest of the action. Accusing the Swatow craft of participating in the attack was no "solution"; in fact, it only added to the confusion. In reality, though, this statement by NSA was a vain attempt to cover the problem of the contradictory report from Phu Bai. It was nothing but speculation – ignorant speculation at that. Furthermore, this summary report still did not address the issue of the total lack of intercept of any North Vietnamese attack command and control communications.

(U) Fingering the Swatows as the culprits only made the "attack" scenario more improbable for another reason. The distance from Quang Khe naval base (17°46'N, 106°29'E) to the reported first radar plot by the Maddox, forty to forty-five nautical miles northeast of its position, is about 120 nautical miles. However, this distance should not be construed as a "straight line" dash from

Quang Khe. Because the DRV boats were "detected" coming from the east, they would have had to travel in a long arc northward and then southeast around the American destroyers which were speeding to the southeast. Also, remember that the Maddox and Turner Joy did not "detect" these boats until they approached from the east, so the route to the north of the American destroyers had to be at a distance sufficient to avoid discovery by radar. This lengthens to a distance of around 180 nautical miles. Since the "attack order" was issued at 1115Z and the initial radar plot was at 1336Z (and we are presuming that the postulated boats left at the exact time of the first intercept, or were soon under way at the time), then the boats would have had to have been traveling at a speed of nearly seventy miles per hour (about 110 kph) to have been where the Maddox first detected them – at a rate some 58 percent higher than the Swatow's known top speed!

(U) The only other base from which the "attack" could have been staged was Port Wallut, which was the base for the P-4 Squadron 135. The distance from Port Wallut (21°13'N, 107°34'E) to the initial point of detection by the Desoto radars is about 140 nautical miles. However, the same problem exists here as for Quang Khe, though not quite as extreme, for the P-4s. The scenario presumes that they would have been moving at a little less than seventy miles per hour, or a good 40 percent higher than the boat's listed maximum speed.

(S//SI) Another possibility to consider when looking at the "attack message" is that there was some other activity to which the "military operations" (if that is the interpretation one could have) might have referred. In fact, there was something else going on that night of 4/5 August which is seldom mentioned in the public record: a maritime OPLAN-34A mission was, in fact, moving northward along the DRV coastline at the time when the American destroyers were shooting away at those radar returns. The Marolda and Fitzgerald history of the U.S. Navy in Vietnam fails to mention the ongoing 34A mission. Official Washington as well never mentioned this 34A mission. In classified hearings in February 1968, Secretary of Defense McNamara never mentioned this mission, claiming that the last one prior to the 4 August attack occurred on the night of 3-4 August. Obviously, if the 34A mission of the night of 4-5 August were known at the time, it would have undercut Washington's claim that nothing else was happening that night which might have provoked Hanoi.

(U) This 34A mission had been scheduled back at the end of July by COMUSMACV, which then had informed Washington of the missions planned for all of August. This particular foray's main objective was the shelling of the island of Hon Matt. It is not certain when this mission left Danang, though it was normal for the boats to depart in the late afternoon to take advantage of darkness by the time they reached the DRV coastline. So a departure time between 1500G and 1600G (0900Z) would not be too far off.

(S//SI) At 2316G (1616Z) the Marine mission at Phu Bai intercepted a message from the DRV naval HQ in Haiphong to T-142 that six enemy raiding vessels had been located somewhere south of Thanh Hoa (20°00′N, 105°30′E). (The actual position is confusing due to a garble in the text transmitted from Phu Bai. Neither the time of the enemy boats' position nor their course is clear.)[119] This intercept occurred only a few minutes before the JCS approved an urgent recall order from CINCPACFLT for the 34A mission to be discontinued and return to Danang immediately.[120] It is possible that the Kit Kat support element may have passed this intelligence to the MACV/SOG, which in turn began the recall.

(S//SI) In light of what finally transpired with T-142 and the two P-4 torpedo boats, it seems that they were not part of an defensive plan against the raiders. That this Swatow received the message about the raiders does not seem odd in light of the fact that T-142 seems to have served

as some sort of radio relay for other boats or as a communications guard vessel for all DRV naval operations: a majority of intercepted messages during the period seem to have been sent to or through T-142. From other intercepts, we know that at least another Swatow, T-379, was near Hon Matt; two others, T-130 and T-132, were near Hon Me Island; and T-165 had deployed, as well. If the DRV was planning to attack the 34A raiders on 4 August, these craft would have been the logical ones to use because of their substantial deck gun armament. However, no other communications activity related to any other Swatow patrol craft was intercepted that night. So it remains uncertain what, if anything, Hanoi was planning to do to fend off the 34A mission of 4 August.

(S//SI) Exhibit B: The Lack of Vietnamese Command, Control, Communications, and Intelligence

(S//SI) To our initial question as to who was involved in the apparent attack of the two American destroyers, we must add a corollary question: How did the North Vietnamese carry out the "attack"; that is, how were the boats controlled and vectored to the American ships? If we recall the three elements of the command, control, communications and intelligence (C3I) observed during the previous two days' activities – communications from Haiphong and Port Wallut, relayed through the Swatow-class boats; the relay of tracking information on the American ships; and the use of the Skin Head surface search radar – then we have another serious problem with the engagement of the night of 4 August because none of these elements was present during the so-called attack.

(S//SI) During the entire day of 4 August, most of the communications intercepted from either DRV naval command entities in Port Wallut or Haiphong either were directed to the craft involved in the salvage and recovery of the two Squadron 135 torpedo boats, or else were relays of tracking reports of the Desoto patrol, and those latter messages were exchanged with T-142, which was involved in the ongoing recovery operations. The only other messages which were intercepted contained orders for other *Swatow*-class patrol boats to move to positions along the coast: T-130 and T-132 were ordered to Hon Me Island, while T-165 was ordered to leave Haiphong at 1448G (0748Z) and move to the entrance of an unspecified bay.[121]

(S//SI) During the 2 August attack, there were elements of high-level control from the naval commands at Port Wallut and Haiphong, both of whom sent orders and tracking reports to the attacking boats. The *Swatow*s, principally T-142, acted as a communications relay between the torpedo boats and the onshore commands. The messages were transmitted using high frequency manual morse communications which were intercepted throughout the day, even during the fighting. Finally, there were sporadic boat-to-boat VHF, tactical voice communications which the intercept positions aboard the *Maddox*'s hut could intercept, at least until the destroyer activated its fire control radars, which interfered with the navy's monitoring.

(S//SI) However, not one of these elements was detected during the night of 4 August. Trying to find more evidence of the purported attack, NSA had queried the NSG detachment aboard the *Maddox* on 6 August to supply urgently all intercept that "PROVIDES PROOF OF DRV ATTACK ON FOUR AUGUST UPON U.S. NAVAL VESSELS."[122] Within five hours came the disheartening reply from the DSU. There was no manual morse intercept to prove the DRV attack of 4 August. Furthermore, voice intercept was nil, except for signal checks between two unidentified stations.[123]

(S//SI) The tracking messages locating the Desoto patrol ships had been intercepted by the Americans early in the day of 4 August. However, the last credible position of the American ships was passed at 1610G (0910Z) from Haiphong to T-142. The position, 19°36'N, 106°19'E, was fairly close to the Desoto patrol's position at the time. This was just about two hours before Herrick ordered his ships to head east in reaction to the Phu Bai Critic.[124] However, it should be pointed out that this position report was sent to the T-142, which was involved in the salvage of the two torpedo boats. There is no evidence that the T-142 relayed it to any other boat or command.

(S//SI) One more position report on the Desoto patrol was sent from Port Wallut to a probable vessel at 2246G (1546Z), which was about an hour after the supposed engagement had begun. This position report might seem as related to the action, except for two problems. First of all, the report located the American ships thirty-five nautical miles east of Hon Matt Island, which places the destroyers some eighty nautical miles northwest of where they actually were at the time! In addition, the report does not carry the time associated with the Americans' position. (The reported location suggests, however, at least from the track the Desoto patrol took that night, that this position report was about four to five hours old.) So, this information could hardly be used by any North Vietnamese boats intending to attack the Americans. Secondly, the message includes an order (or advisory) to the recipient to maintain a continuous communications watch with an unidentified entity, as well as to "go close to shore."[125] This latter command seems to be hardly intended for boats looking to attack the American ships; rather it appears suited for the boats involved in the salvage operations or the other patrol boats spread out along the DRV coast.

(S//SI) The issue of DRV tracking of the Desoto patrol is important. For in September 1964 NSA would release a report on Vietnamese coastal radar operations during the period. In this report, NSA would contend that active tracking by the coastal observation posts equipped with coastal surveillance radars would indicate hostile intentions by Hanoi. The report pointed out that there was no tracking of the *Craig* earlier in March.[126] This was not quite true: the DRV was aware of the location of the destroyer, but its time off the Vietnamese coast was quite short so the tracking was spotty.

(S//SI) The same report also pointed out that the *Maddox* was under "constant" radar surveillance before it came under attack on 2 August. However, the report then ducks the issue of the observed sporadic tracking by the North Vietnamese on 4 August with the claim that "The evidence is still inconclusive in light of the virtual absence of trackings on 3-4 August before the second attack."[127] The evidence would never be found. The final report from the DSU aboard the *Maddox* showed only occasional coastal tracking from shore stations and North Vietnamese boats on 4 August. And it had ended by mid-afternoon.[128]

(S) Finally, the Americans detected no Skin Head emissions during the "attack" on 4 August. Keep in mind that during 3 August the DRV boats that shadowed the Desoto patrol used their Skin Head surface search radars, and that these emissions were detected by the ELINT position in the intercept hut aboard the *Maddox*. These signals were also intercepted during the morning and early afternoon of 4 August.[129]

(S//SI) While it is true that no North Vietnamese radar emissions were detected during the 2 August attack on the *Maddox*, it must be remembered that this attack occurred in the daytime under nearly ideal conditions.[130] Yet, the DRV boats had initial difficulty visually locating and then following the *Maddox*. What we are confronted with in the second "attack" is the proposition that the North Vietnamese boats themselves, which the *Turner Joy* and *Maddox* detected using only their radars, could find the Americans so far out at sea (over 100 nautical miles), in heavy swells (three to six feet), at night, with a low cloud cover, *without using their*

radars. Even if the North Vietnamese had the equipment to receive the American radar pulses, this information would have given them only a crude bearing on which to track. They could not determine distance, speed, or anything else with which to plot any sort of torpedo attack.[131] Besides that, how could they even begin to track the American ships when the latest valid position was almost five hours old!

(U) In the Sherlock Holmes story "Silver Blaze," the great Victorian detective and his assistant, Dr. Watson, are confronted with the paradox of a crime which cannot be proven to have happened. In the story there is this exchange:

> Is there any point to which you wish to draw my attention?
> To the curious incident of the dog in the night-time.
> The dog did nothing in the night-time.
> That was the curious incident, remarked Sherlock Holmes.[132]

(S//SI) And so it is with the 4 August incident: there were no DRV naval communications or radar emissions which were normally associated with a naval engagement. Just two days prior, the Americans had an opportunity to observe Vietnamese naval communications during the attack on the *Maddox*. Among other things, they had seen that the Vietnamese had difficulties in setting up and maintaining control of an attack, as the incident with the conflicting orders illustrated. And so there should have been a generous amount of intercept of any communications which would have supported the claims of the two American destroyers.

(S//SI) Yet, nothing as much as a single bark was intercepted. As Holmes would come to conclude that no crime was committed, so we must conclude that, since U.S. SIGINT never intercepted anything associated with an attack, none ever occurred. And the contention that all possible communications and emissions reflecting an attack might have gone unheard can be dismissed. As Gerrel Moore, the officer-in-charge of the DSU on board the *Maddox*, observed: "I can't believe that somebody wouldn't have picked up something."[133] Finally, a review of the DSU intercept log for 4 August showed no variation in Vietnamese communications procedures which could suggest that any change or changes, such as new operating frequencies, callsigns, or procedures, were implemented just for the "attack" that could elude American intercept.[134]

(S//SI) Exhibit C: The "After-Action" Report

(S//SI) With there being no SIGINT evidence of an attack, and the rest of the evidence from visual, radar, and sonar sources so unsupportive, we are left with attempting to explain the intercept of late 4 August, which was interpreted as an after-action report. Remember, it was this intercept which was so critical to McNamara's contention that an attack had occurred – two of the five pieces of his list of "convincing" evidence. Yet, when we look closely at the intercept, there are four major problems with the assertion that it was a report on the supposed engagement from just a few hours earlier on 4 August. The translation, "T10-64," issued by NSA at 1933Z on 4 August (0233G, 5 August) is shown on this page.

(S//SI) The first difficulty with the intercept is that it does not resemble an after-action report of the type which had been intercepted early on 3 August by the Marine element at Phu Bai. That intercept, sent by T-142 to T-146 and the Port Wallut HQ of Squadron 135, contained a chronology of events beginning at 0925G on 2 August when T-146 met the three boats from Squadron 135 and guided them to Hon Me Island. The report noted that the attack against the Americans began at 1525G, and that by 1625G, all the boats had received the orders to break off the attack.[135]

(S//SI) In the 4 August translation, there is no chronology associated with the supposed down-

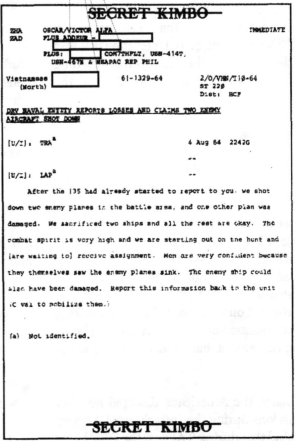

SECRET KIMBO

ZHA ZAD	OSCAR/VICTOR ALFA PLUS ADDRESS –			IMMEDIATE
	PLUS:		CON7THFLT, USS-414T, USN-467N & NSAPAC REP PHIL	
Vietnamese (North)		61-1329-64	2/0/VHN/T10-64 ST 220 Dist: BCP	

DRV NAVAL ENTITY REPORTS LOSSES AND CLAIMS TWO ENEMY AIRCRAFT SHOT DOWN

[U/I]: TRA(a)   4 Aug 64 2242G

                                        --

[U/I]: LAP(a)   --

    After the 135 had already started to report to you, we shot down two enemy planes in the battle area, and one other plan was damaged. We sacrificed two ships and all the rest are okay. The combat spirit is very high and we are starting out on the hunt and [are waiting to] receive assignment. Men are very confident because they themselves saw the enemy planes sink. The enemy ship could also have been damaged. Report this information back to the unit [C vai to mobilize them.]

(a) Not identified.

SECRET KIMBO

(S//SI) The supposed Vietnamese communist naval after-action report

ing of the aircraft. There is no mention of any participating boats or units, except to mention that two were "SACRIFICED . . . AND ALL THE REST ARE OKAY." The only sense of when anything happened comes with the beginning phrase, "AFTER THE 135 HAD ALREADY STARTED TO REPORT TO YOU." In fact, the entire report seems incoherent, not the type one expected to see sent by an officer on the scene, as had been intercepted on 3 August. It rambles, mixing morale boosting statements with seemingly repetitious references to planes being shot down and then seeing them "sink."

(S//SI) Secondly, there is a problem with the translation of a critical passage: "WE SACRIFICED TWO SHIPS AND ALL THE REST ARE

OKAY." Unfortunately, the original, decrypted Vietnamese language version of the message cannot be located in the NSA Archives. Also, a possible original translation of the entire message (or part of it), numbered "T162-64" and issued by the navy site at San Miguel, cannot be found in the NSA Archives file of that site's 1964 translations. Without either document, we are left with the conjecture of what Vietnamese words were seen by the navy analysts and linguists at San Miguel and their counterparts at NSA.

(S//SI) However, from the existing records, what we do know is that the translation finally issued by NSA was *not* what was initially reported by San Miguel. At 1550Z (2250G) on 4 August, when the American destroyers were shooting away at those radar returns, San Miguel intercepted a message which it identified as being sent from T-142 to an unidentified entity at My Duc (19°52'N, 105°57'E). In total, the report, numbered "R38," read:

> WE SHOT AT TWO ENEMY AIRPLANES AND AT LEAST ONE WAS DAMAGED. WE SACRIFICED TWO COMRADES BUT ALL ARE BRAVE AND RECOGNIZE OUR OBLIGATION. [136]

(U) How the translation changed from "comrades" in the San Miguel version to "boats" in the NSA version is unknown. Edwin Moise, in his study of the Tonkin Gulf, suggests that a Vietnamese sentence to the effect of losing two comrades could hardly be construed to mean two ships: "HAI DONG CHI HY SINH" or "HAI DONG CHI BI HY SINH" are possible Vietnamese phrases which could be translated to "sacrificing two comrades."[137] The Vietnamese word for boat, "TAU," had been seen in earlier intercepted messages. This would be consistent, since Hanoi's messages usually shortened the word to just the letter "T" from where the same letter designators for Hanoi's boats comes from, such as "T-142," "T-146," etc.

(S//SI) A possible argument that there was a garble in the encryption of the message which could have led to confusion does not hold.

(U) There is an additional point of interest: President Johnson in his memoirs noted that "The North Vietnamese skipper reported that his unit had 'sacrificed two comrades'. " Our *experts* said that this meant *either* two enemy *boats* or two *men* in the attack group."[139] (My italics in all cases.) This is an interesting admission, for it suggests, and rather strongly, that even the day that the NSA translation was issued, the intercept was considered, at best, ambiguous in its meaning. Why NSA opted for "boats" instead of "comrades" in its final translation is not clear, especially if the difference was enough to tell the president.

(S//SI) The third problem is with the time of the intercept and the file time listed on the NSA translation. The file time, 2242G (1542Z), is barely one hour after the *Turner Joy* and *Maddox* opened fire on the first radar returns. As we saw with the messages from 2 August, this entry is the time that the Vietnamese communications center (or a radio operator) assigned to the message when it arrived ready for transmission, which, as it turns out, in this case took another eight minutes to complete. If we allow any time for the

(b)(1)
(b)(3)-50 USC 403
(b)(3)-18 USC 798
(b)(3)-P.L. 86-36

message's drafting, coordination, and encryption (remember, this is a manual system with three charts), then the actual time of the composition of the message must be pushed back close to the beginning of the so-called engagement. Even if we are generous with our appreciation of the skill of the Vietnamese communications personnel in encrypting the message, we still have to concede some time to get the message from composition to transmission. The more time we allow for this process, then the closer its origin comes up to the time that the destroyers first opened fire. In that case, then, the intercept cannot be considered an after-action report of the events currently occurring at sea in the Gulf of Tonkin.

(S//SI) The question of the time of origin for the information in the Vietnamese message gets even more suspect when we consider the identities of the Vietnamese who may have sent and received it. The NSA translation carries the two callwords "TRA" and "LAP" as unidentified. Actually, this is not true. San Miguel, in its reports, identified the transmitting station, known by the covername "TRA," as the T-142 patrol boat. The receiving station, "LAP," was identified as a shore station at My Duc, possibly the coastal observation post which earlier had tracked the American ships.[140]

(S//SI) In reality, these equations probably were incorrect. The probable identities for the covernames had been known for some time; it is just that San Miguel confused them. "TRA" had been associated with a DRV naval HQs in Haiphong as recently as 2 August. "LAP" had been identified with T-142 on 30 July.[141] However, the exact identities are not important. What is critical is that Haiphong could not have originated the information in the intercept; it had to come from some other source. Another station had to compose a report, encrypt, and transmit the information to Haiphong before it could, in turn, send its message. This means that the very first version of this "after-action" report probably

was composed at or before the time the two destroyers opened fire!

(S//SI) The message file time, 2242G (1542Z) and the intercept time, 1550Z (2250G), should have been highlighted in the translation. These times would have indicated that the intercept could not have been construed as an after-action report. Neither critical time element was noted in the translation. Instead, it seems that the time NSA released the translation, 1933Z (or 1955Z if it had been relayed), was the critical element. That the translation was issued some two and one-half hours after the incident was over probably was the reason it was interpreted by its Washington recipients as a North Vietnamese after-action report.

(S//SI) The translation as issued is hardly helpful in providing a useful background to explain its significance. The title, "DRV NAVAL ENTITY REPORTS LOSSES AND CLAIMS TWO ENEMY AIRCRAFT SHOT DOWN," does not indicate any context for the translation. That being so, it would not be difficult to infer that the translation referred to the recently ended combat action. So, it just hung there waiting for someone to claim it, and the Johnson administration jumped on it. Remember, this translation arrived in Washington midway in the afternoon of 4 August just at the time that the administration was trying to resolve the doubts about the attack that Captain Herrick had reported. And, as we have seen, it was to be the answer to all of the lingering doubts as to the validity of the attack. NSA itself would use the translation to support the contention that there had been a second attack as well, quoting excerpts from it in several Gulf of Tonkin Summary reports issued from 4 to 6 August. The problem with the file and intercept times is a critical one, and it reflects a failure by the analysts who issued the translation to draw attention to them.

(S//SI) Yet, it is the fourth problem with the translation which is the most troublesome: that is, specifically, how it was put together. It was mentioned above that the original intercept of the translation was missing from NSA files on the Gulf of Tonkin. We also mentioned that the possible English translation of the entire or part of the intercept, "T162-64," issued by San Miguel, was missing. This situation is odd since crucial earlier and original intercepts, such as the "attack message" and several tracking reports, were available and placed in the allegedly "complete" NSA chronology of the attacks, the latter document of which we will discuss shortly. But neither the original intercept nor the translations from San Miguel are in the chronology. It would seem that they should be there to buttress the validity of the all-important "after-action" report.[142] However, they are not; therein lies the problem.

(S//SI) For only four minutes (1554Z) after San Miguel reported the transmission about "sacrificing two comrades," it published the following intercept from T-142 to My Duc:

((3 GR G)) THE NEWS [BECAU[S]E] THEY DID CONTINUOUSLY SEE WITH THEIR OWN EYES ENEMY AIRCRAFT FALL INTO THE SEA. ENEMY VESSEL PERHAPS IS DAMAGED. REPORT THIS NEWS TO THE MOBILIZED UNIT.[143]

(S//SI) If we take the two intercepts from San Miguel in the sequence in which they were monitored and put them together, we have constructed, with the addition of some transitional words, the so-called "after-action" translation, "T-10," issued by NSA at 1933Z on 4 August. Since the messages were transmitted by the Vietnamese in this sequence, both spoke of aircraft, and were transmitted shortly after one another with little or no interval, it probably was not difficult to conflate the two as parts of the same message.

(S//SI) However, are these two intercepts really parts of the same message? The answer turns out to be no. This is because the English translation of the second intercept exists. San

Miguel transmitted it to NSA on 8 August as part of the post-crisis review. It carried an important item — the Vietnamese-assigned message file number, "NR24," which indicates that the second intercept was a separate message after all, and not part of the first intercept![144]

(S//SI) So, if we look at the NSA translation, "T10," specifically beginning at the phrase "BECAUSE THEY THEMSELVES SAW. . . ." to the end, what we actually are looking at is a separate North Vietnamese message. The reason for two messages is easy to explain. The second one is reporting what the Vietnamese observed of the 4 August action from either one of their boats near the coast, or coastal installations.[145] What the Vietnamese actually saw was either the flares dropped by the carrier Ticonderoga's aircraft to illuminate the DRV boats they were told were there by the two destroyers, or any of the fifty or so starshells fired by the two American ships to illuminate targets. Note that the second intercept reports only that "ENEMY AIRCRAFT FALLING INTO THE SEA." There is no mention by the Vietnamese of shooting at them, as we would expect if it were an report after an engagement with the Americans as there is in the first intercept. In the same fashion, the flashes from the destroyers' guns and shells exploding observed from over the horizon must have suggested to the Vietnamese that one of the American ships had been hit. San Miguel's analysts recognized that the second intercept dealt with that evening's actions. San Miguel, then, reported it first at 1632Z, while the first intercept about "sacrificing comrades" was reported later at 1646Z.

(S//SI) If we again look at the first intercept from San Miguel, we note that the Vietnamese claim they shot at two planes and damaged one. This happens to be in line with their later claims from the action on 2 August. Additionally, the loss of two comrades probably refers to the casualties suffered by T-336 from the same day's fighting.[146] (Keep in mind that the whereabouts and condition of T-339 were unknown to the

DRV command as late as 4 August. It was still considered sunk.)

(U) The congruence of the NSA and the San Miguel reports has been noted elsewhere. In Edwin Moise's book on the Tonkin Gulf, he discusses the resemblance between a "longer" message and a "shorter" one he had received from NSA in response to a FOIA request. Since he had received heavily redacted versions of "T10" and "R38" and "R39" from San Miguel, it was difficult for him to determine the critical fact that the two reports from the Philippines were issued before the NSA translation. However, he did catch the similarity among them, especially the phrases about the downed planes.[147]

(S//SI) This finding that San Miguel had issued two separate reports, which probably had been conflated into a single translation by NSA, may explain the description by President Johnson of the discussions with the so-called technical experts at the White House the afternoon of the attack. The major point that Johnson related was the explanation that the expression "sacrificing two comrades" could have meant two enemy boats or two men. The fact that this issue was brought up strongly suggests that the reports from San Miguel probably were circulating among intelligence and defense officials, and that questions were being raised as to which version was correct, the boats or the comrades. But it is still not clear from this incident what the source was of the NSA version which claimed that two boats were lost instead of two men. As we stated earlier, without the original Vietnamese text, we are left with conjecture. However, with the great divergence between the reports issued by San Miguel and NSA, attention must fall primarily on the actions of the NSA analysts. Why did they change San Miguel's original translation?

(S//SI) This analysis of the NSA translation of the so-called after-action report may appear excessive. Yet it is warranted because of the crucial role played by it in convincing the Johnson administration of the validity of the claim that the two destroyers indeed had been attacked by the North Vietnamese. The critical analysis of the translation has revealed several problems with the text itself, the context and timing of the intercept, that is, whether it was really related to the attack, and finally, the circumstances of the original analysis of the intercept.

(S//SI) If the results of this analysis of the translation were not enough to make one suspect its validity, the difficulties with the documentary source record undermine it all the more. For the sources we do not have, that is, the missing technical supplements and the translation, "T162," leave us with a serious gap: we have only the two field reports and single NSA English translation. The differences between the field version and the one published by NSA are too large to ignore; depending on which translation one accepts, the possible interpretations of the incident of 4 August are either that nothing happened or that there was an attack.

(U) Exhibit D: A Matter of Certainty

(U) A question remains, What were the circumstances surrounding the issuance of this last translation? The answer is that we do not exactly know the details of how it was put together. However, we do have some clues as to the environment in which the analysis reporting by NSA was done.

(S//SI) After the 2 August attack, the analytic division concerned with the North Vietnamese problem, B26, had established an informal twenty-four-hour watch center to handle the SIGINT reporting from the Gulf of Tonkin. A relatively small team, perhaps fewer than ten, of analysts, linguists, and supervisory personnel, staffed the center. Unfortunately, there were what can be called "environmental pressures" on the staff. Notably, a crisis atmosphere surrounding everyone and everything, which, combined with twelve- to sixteen-hour days, probably led to serious problems of pressure and fatigue. There was also the problem that the linguists available were relatively inexperienced, some being barely a year or two removed from language school. Besides just reviewing the field intercept, people from this crisis cell also briefed the Pentagon and National Security Council.[148]

(S//SI) It appears that there was little in the way of control or interaction between this cell and senior NSA leadership. The director, NSA, General Blake, was out of town at the time. The various briefings at the Pentagon, and possibly the White House, were handled by mid-level managers and staffers operating out of the crisis cell and NSA liaison positions in the Pentagon and the White House. In fact, for the most part, it seems that senior NSA leadership stayed out of the proceedings, exercising little control or oversight.[149]

(U) That there might have been a lot of pressure on the NSA people to produce "proof" is quite likely. Regarding that charged period, Ray Cline, the former CIA deputy director, recalled that "Everybody was demanding the sigint (signals intelligence; intercepts); they wanted it quick, they didn't want anybody to take any time to analyze it." [150] It was certainly a crisis moment. We know from the chronology mentioned earlier, that the translation of the "after-action" report arrived about two hours after the time that the first news of Captain Herrick's doubts about the action had arrived in Washington. Also, as we have seen, McNamara's evidence contained at least two points from the NSA translation. Of this, there is little to doubt. However, it remains a question as to whether the analysts and managers in NSA were certain of the second attack.

(S//SI) It has been reported in other histories that the NSA analyst (or analysts) who actually decrypted and translated the intercepts were doubtful of the second incident from the very beginning, believing that the message referred to

the 2 August attack.[151] Furthermore, a review of oral histories suggests that in the watch center there was a sort of division between those who were certain the second attack occurred, which was composed of mid-level management, and the analysts who were not so sure.[152]

(S//SI) Actually, the doubters were not as skeptical about the reality of the attack as much as they as were uncertain as how to label the intercept about the Vietnamese shooting at/down the aircraft. Was it related to what was happening in the Gulf of Tonkin? As one linguist recalled, the problem came down to "Was this, or was this not?" The deciding element for the analysts was the fact that the intercept time (1550Z or 1559Z) of the "after action" intercept *coincided* with the time frame of the attack on the two destroyers: an analytic "coin toss" was made, and the translation went out which was interpreted as supporting the validity of the second attack.[153] There was no explicit connection between the intercept and events: it was inferred from the coincidence of the time of the intercept and the time of the ongoing "attack." Also implicit in this decision was a lack of confidence concerning the validity of the information; it could not stand by itself as the evidence, at least in the minds of the analysts.

(U) On such small things as a mental "coin toss," then, does history often turn.

(S//SI) As to the nature of the translation, according to the same linguist, reportedly there were no enforced "word changes" in this report (or any others which were issued), though arguments over translation "styles" did occur. These arguments were over the rendering of the translations from the Vietnamese original "into suitable English." [154]

(TS//SI) This analysis by coin flip left the door open for follow-up reports which more openly supported the notion of an attack. Barely six hours after it issued the "after-action" translation, NSA released its first summary report of the action. This summary contained quotes from the earlier after-action translation. These quotes were placed in summary in such a way as to substantiate collateral radar, sonar, and visual information from the Desoto patrol. On 6 August two more summaries were released by NSA which carried more SIGINT which the Agency asserted supported the second attack scenario. Publicly, at least, and probably from the very beginning, NSA supported the Johnson administration's claim for a second attack.[155] These reports are important in understanding the post-attack position taken by NSA.

(S//SI) As for the doubts about the second attack among the analysts at NSA, it appears that none of them were ever publicized during the briefings with officials at the Defense Department. Or, if they were mentioned, they were downplayed. In fact, it seems that the NSA position was a fairly straightforward one: that the second attack occurred.[156] So firm was NSA's position, that one previous NSA historian has suggested that this allowed President Johnson to shift the blame for the final decision from himself to the "experts" who had assured him of the strength of the evidence from the SIGINT.[157]

(U) Officially, everyone else in Washington supported the notion that there had been an attack. Later statements by various intelligence and Defense Department officials suggest that there was a large group who simply did not believe that the attack had happened or that the evidence even pointed to an attack. Many high-ranking officials from CIA, the Department of State, and the Pentagon could not see the evidence assembled by McNamara as supporting a Vietnamese attack. Some of them were skeptical (or claim to have been so) from almost the beginning of the incident. This group of doubters included the then U.S. Army's deputy chief of staff for military operations, General Bruce Palmer Jr., Ray Cline, the CIA's deputy director for intelligence, the heads of the Department of State's Intelligence and Far Eastern Divisions, as

well as a host of staffers on the National Security Council and in the Defense Department, who, in years to come, would become notable: Daniel Ellsberg, Alvid Friedman, and Alexander Haig.

(U) Yet, despite doubts, people in the intelligence and defense communities kept their silence. As much as anything else, it was an awareness that President Johnson would brook no uncertainty that could undermine his position. Faced with this attitude, Ray Cline was quoted as saying: ". . . we knew it was bum dope that we were getting from the Seventh Fleet, but we were told only to give the facts with no elaboration on the nature of the evidence. Everyone knew how volatile LBJ was. He did not like to deal with uncertainties." [158]

(S//SI) And there were plenty of people in NSA and the cryptologic community who doubted that the SIGINT was convincing evidence of an attack. Notable among these were the chief of B Group, who seems to have been skeptical from the morning of 5 August, and the NSA Pacific Representative (NSAPAC), who sent a message to DIRNSA listing his doubts after reviewing a CINCPAC study of the affair.[159]

(TS//SI) With all of the doubters about the attack, whether they were uncertain from the beginning, or saw the problems with the "evidence" later on, it is surprising that what emerged from various intelligence and Defense Department studies of the 4 August event were even more confirmations that the attack had occurred. Within weeks of the event, teams from the navy commands in the Pacific region, CINCPAC and Seventh Fleet, conducted reviews which verified the attack. A Defense Department team arrived in mid-August and conducted interviews of the pilots and the crews of the destroyers. They found strong evidence for the attack as well.[160] The Joint Reconnaissance Center issued a chronology of events, while ASA Pacific Headquarters conducted a critique of the reporting by Phu Bai during SIGINT Readiness Bravo Lantern, the enhanced SIGINT coverage ordered during the Gulf of Tonkin crisis.[161] Both documents supported the idea of a second attack.

(S//SI) Exhibit E: And Some More Silent Dogs

(S//SI) Various elements of the Naval Security Group, which oversaw and provided the manning for the Desoto missions, issued reports on the incidents in the Gulf of Tonkin which were strangely reticent about the evidence of the attack on the night of the 4th. For example, in the report issued by the commanding officer of NSG detachment aboard the *Maddox*, two and one-half pages are devoted to SIGINT reflections of the 2 August attack. The follow-up air strikes of 5 August warrant another half page. Yet the statement summarizing the SIGINT activity of 4 August is rendered in just in one sentence:

> H. On 4 August information received from USN 414T and USM 626J [Phu Bai] indicated a possible attack on the Desoto ships by the DRV naval vessels.[162]

(S//SI) A report from the director, Naval Security Group Pacific, of 24 August was similar. Twelve paragraphs of the message are devoted in recounting the SIGINT detail of the 2 August attacks. The recounting of the "attack" of 4 August was done in a short entry of two paragraphs, the first of which contained the information that T-142 was "again shadowing" the U.S. ships. It also refers to "moderately heavy tracking" by two DRV tracking sites at Thanh Hoa (20°00′N, 105°30′E) and Hon En (18°18′N, 106°09′E)." The site at Than Hoa would have tracked the two ships early on 4 August, but the attack was several hours later. When Hon En tracked the ships is unknown. The second paragraph mentions only the two reports from Phu Bai, stating that they indicated "a possible attack." [163]

(S//SI) Further evidence, and perhaps one of the strongest pieces available indicating that no attack had happened, came from the North Vietnamese themselves. On 6 August, an unidentified DRV naval entity, possibly the naval HQ at Port Wallut, transmitted to an unidentified station a recap of the previous combat with the Americans. It summarized the events of 2 August and mentioned their boats fighting the "American warship." It also recounted that their naval and air defense forces had shot down some American warplanes on 5 August and had captured one American pilot alive. Yet, there is no mention of anything occurring on the night of 4 August in this recap.[164] The absence of any reference to 4 August cannot be attributed to North Vietnamese embarrassment over the results of the "action"; they lost heavily on both 2 and 5 August. The only conclusion that this intercept points to is that there was no attack on the night of 4 August.

(S//SI) Oddly, this last intercept has never been used in any evaluation of the Gulf of Tonkin incidents. Understandably, those evaluations have tended to rely on the evidence from the time period of the incidents themselves. Surely, a North Vietnamese accounting of the operations for the previous three days would have been considered as part of the body of evidence concerning the attack. Yet it was not used, although NSA summaries issued on the same day were. Was that because the intercept says nothing about an attack on 4 August?

(S//SI) Maintaining the Line: The NSA Summary Reports and the "Del Lang Chronology"

(S//SI) As the field sites submitted their reports on what intercept they did or did not have, as in the case of the NSG element aboard the *Maddox*, and the analysts had the luxury of time to review all of the SIGINT, the various evaluations they produced continued to reflect the official position that the second attack had occurred. The most important early response from Fort Meade was a series of summary reports issued between 5 and 7 August. It is these reports which make up first official NSA judgment on what happened. Because of this, they deserve a close look, since they establish the tone and form for the later chronology, which became, in a way, the final NSA statement on what had happened.

(TS//SI) NSA issued five summary and situation reports after the incident, beginning early on 5 August. Of the five, numbers "R01" through "R05," the pertinent ones are the first three, especially the first and third. These three reports explicitly state that the 4 August attack occurred. Report "R01" notes that the reports from the destroyer that it had sunk two torpedo boats were later "confirmed by a DRV message which stated 'that we had sacrificed two ships and the rest are okay'." [165] Where this idea that two boats were sunk came from is hard to say. NSA received all messages from the Desoto patrol via the JCS. All through the afternoon of 4 August, the destroyers reported at first that three boats had been sunk, then later changed it to one sunk and one, possibly two, damaged.[166] The second post-incident report, known as "Gulf of Tonkin SIGINT Situation Report No. 1," included the statement "following the 4 August attack."

(TS//SI) It was the third report that was the most open in supporting the idea of the second attack. It was stated in the lead sentence of the report that "This report is a summary of those DRV naval communications during the period 1-5 August which demonstrate irrefutably that DRV naval boats did, in fact, engage in preplanned combat against U.S. destroyers patrolling in international waters." [167]

(TS//SI) However, the confident tone of the third report is belied by its thin layer of evidence. And this problem was noticed by some of its recipients. Late on the afternoon of 6 August, a DIA representative queried NSA if additional SIGINT was available from the 4 August incident. He reported that Secretary McNamara was not satisfied with the contents of this third summary report, "that it was insufficient for his purposes." In reviewing the SIGINT from the incident, it was discovered that there was a large gap with no intercept – specifically, the time leading up to the actual attack. Based on this discovery, urgent messages were sent to the field sites requesting all intercept.[168] And, as we have seen, the field sites had nothing else to add.

(TS//SI) There are problems with the way this series of reports portrays the information in them. For example, the first report mentions the salvage operations of the two damaged DRV torpedo boats which had been discussed earlier. However, unlike what we discovered, the summary does not go on to report that these operations continued into the time of the attack as reported by the marines at Phu Bai. The authors of the third report tried to address this with the speculation that the attacking boats might have come from Quang Khe or some other base in the DRV Southern Command.[169] But this has already been shown to be wrong since the distance traveled for the boats to have attacked from the east could not have been accomplished because of the limitations of the boats' speed.

(TS//SI) Perhaps the most serious problem, though, is the lack of any citation of source reports which made up the summaries. This is a critical point, since the information referred to in the summaries is coming from already published, serialized NSA and field site reports and translations. The very lack of notes is odd since this type of summary reporting required that source notes be included. It seems that if the Agency was attempting to build a case demonstrating that an attack had occurred, then the source reports and translations which substantiated the position would have been included. However, this was not the case. In fact, there were cases in which information used in the summaries as evidence, was, in fact, not related at all, or impossible to verify.

(TS//SI) For example, the first summary, "R01," issued early on 5 August, contained this section which strongly suggests that the Desoto patrol was surveyed by DRV aircraft. The entry read:

> During 3 August, DRV Naval Communications reflected the tracking and shadowing of the two destroyers throughout the day; this activity was reported by both destroyers. They were also apparently shadowed by two presumably DRV aircraft. A DRV merchant ship advised its shipping office in Haiphong that 'two bombers' would 'fly' in the direction of the ship and investigate. No further identification of the aircraft was provided.[170]

(TS//SI) This entry was lifted from a San Miguel report on DRV merchant shipping. In it, a single North Vietnamese merchant ship, the *Thong Nhat*, reported that two single-propeller aircraft (*chong chongs*), and not bombers, were flying to investigate the ship, presumably a reference to itself.[171] Hanoi's aircraft inventory contained two single-prop planes – the AN-2 (Colt), a small transport biplane and the YAK-18 (Max) trainer – both of which were unsuitable to maritime patrols. Since the report never specified the nationality of the aircraft, it is likely that they were American A-1H single propeller fighter bombers from the *Ticonderoga*.

(S//SI) At the time of the intercept, 1018Z on 3 August, the Desoto patrol was some sixty miles to the south of the *Thong Nhat*; it seems reasonable that the Desoto combat air patrol would have gone to investigate the North Vietnamese freighter.[172] A few hours after the *Thong Nhat* reported the aircraft, the Haiphong shipping office transmitted an urgent message to three DRV merchant ships to "take precautions against enemy airplanes and ships."[173]

(TS//SI) In addition, the third report, "R03," refers to intercept at 1054Z on 4 August that the DRV was trying to keep "activities under cover" when it was claimed that it had intercepted a message with the sentence "YOU CANNOT PUBLICIZE THE SITUATION OF THE BOATS OF FLOTILLA 135 TO THE BACH DANG."[174] Who is sending this message, and to whom, is not mentioned in the summary. To date, the source of this sentence has not been found; its context, the correctness of the translation, or even its correlation to the attack, cannot be determined.

(TS//SI) Report "R03" also carried another curious entry supporting the idea of an attack. This read "KHOAI HAD MET THE ENEMY." Over the ensuing years this entry bothered people researching the incident. No one could find the original intercept, and no one could seem to explain it.[175] No wonder. The sentence was a rewrite of a San Miguel intercept. The original intercept was of a message from Haiphong to T-146, which originally read: "WHEN ((YOU)) MEET THE ENEMY T333 MUST MOBILIZE." Since the local time of the intercept is 0211G (2011Z) on 5 August, the reference to meeting the enemy has nothing to do with the prior evening's incident. In fact, the tense of the original translation suggests that this was a message anticipating a possible future clash with the Americans, and it was expected that torpedo boat T-333 had to be ready to defend itself.[176] The name "KHOAI" was seen in other intercepts over the prior two days, including the infamous "military operations" one of early 4 August. In reality, "KHOAI" probably was Le Duy Khoai, the commander of Squadron 135. That he, the commanding officer, accompanied Section 3 in its attack against the *Maddox* on 2 August, and stayed on to supervise the recovery operations of his two damaged boats, was standard procedure for DRV naval officers.[177]

(TS//SI) The main NSA effort at producing a record of the events of 2-5 August 1964 centered on a joint postmortem with the Defense Intelligence Agency, begun in late August 1964 and released on 14 October 1964. What was produced was a chronology of events which supported the contention that there had been a second attack. The NSA version of the chronology stayed within the cryptologic community with a very narrow distribution totalling ten recipients. Later, after the second Gulf of Tonkin "incident" of 19 September 1964, a second volume was added to cover that event.[178]

—(TS//SI) This chronology, specifically the volume titled "Chronology of Events of 2-5 August in the Gulf of Tonkin," was bound in a black binder and came to be popularly referred to as the "Del Lang Chronology," named after the B Group staff officer, Lieutenant Colonel Delmar Lang, USAF, who compiled it. Colonel Lang was a veteran cryptologic staff officer with a great deal of liaison experience with various SIGINT missions in Asia, starting with work during the Korean War. He would be instrumental later in implementing various SIGINT support efforts for Rolling Thunder and Linebacker air campaigns. The chronology he produced solidified the official position that the attack had occurred. In the introduction, Lang claimed it to be as complete as far as the SIGINT involvement necessitated. The SIGINT material included product reports, translations, and selected messages between NSA and various field sites and liaison offices. The chronology also made heavy use of non-SIGINT sources, in this case messages from the Desoto patrol, CINCPAC, and the JCS. The chronology was arranged with an introductory time line which highlighted events between 2 to 5 August, followed by the documents which were notated with "tabs" numbered sequentially and cross-referenced in the introduction.[179]

—(S//SI) Like the summaries discussed above, there are serious problems in the chronology with both the amount and subject matter of the SIGINT evidence and the way it is presented. For example, in reference to the 4 August incident, the chronology makes use of only six SIGINT products (not counting the summaries which were a review of published product) as evidence. Now, we have been referring to a large number of these products about the 4 August "attack" throughout this article. All told, between 3 and 6 August, fifty-nine SIGINT products can be identified as being relevant to that purported attack, that is, containing information related in some way to it. These include serialized reports, translations, critics, follow-ups to the Critics, and technical supplements. The fifty-nine products include status reports on the North Vietnamese boats, DRV tracking of the Desoto patrol from coastal observation posts and boats, salvage operations of the damaged boats originally thought to be involved, DRV boat movement and location reports, and intelligence reports. So the six products used in the chronology constitute a bit more than 10 percent of the total available.

—(S//SI) Now, the introduction to the chronology refers to using "representative samples of DIRNSA's COMINT reporting of the activities directly and indirectly related to the situation of the activities in the Gulf of Tonkin."[180] How merely six out of fifty-nine is "representative" is difficult to understand. Furthermore, these six reports are the only ones which can be construed to demonstrate an aggressive intent on the part of Hanoi's navy. They include a 3 August report of a concentration of DRV vessels near Hon Me Island, the three Critics and follow-ups concerning the "attack" being planned for the night of 4 August, the translation of the so-called "after-action" report, and an early 5 August message reporting DRV plans for combat operations on the night of 5 August, which turned out to be related to the ongoing salvage operations.[181]

—(S//SI) None of the other fifty-three products were included in the chronology. These include all of the ones that have been cited earlier in this article, and which demonstrated that no attack was planned, or proved that the North Vietnamese did not know the location of the American destroyers, or indicated that the salvage operations were the primary activity of

Hanoi's navy, or the outright statements in some intercept for the DRV boats to stay away from the Americans. These products were available at the time of the composition of the chronology. Yet why they were not included is unknown. Obviously, their absence leaves the reader with the impression of Hanoi's overt aggression against the American ships.

(S//SI) The way the material is presented is also curious. Almost all of the SIGINT product included for both 2 and 4 August has attached the reproduction of the original intercept of the DRV navy's messages: that is, the cipher and its decrypted Vietnamese text. This allows the reader to see the unfolding of the SIGINT process, from intercept to report.

(S//SI) However, there is one glaring exception to this: the 4 August translation of the so-called "after-action" report used by Secretary McNamara and President Johnson as primary evidence of the attack. In fact, only the translation is included, and it is there only as "a sample." Considering the importance attached to it by the administration, as we saw earlier, this is a very odd way of presenting this piece of critical evidence. It would seem that the NSA originators of the chronology would have added the complete Vietnamese cipher and text to bolster the case for an attack. Yet the translation stands alone. Since we know that the intercept used to produce the translation currently is missing, might we ask if they were already "missing" shortly after the incident itself?

(S//SI) Finally, the chronology does not address the problem of the total lack of North Vietnamese C3I related to the supposed 4 August attack. Not surprisingly, there are samples of the C3I from the 2 August attack. Yet, aside from the so-called "attack" message and the purported "after-action" report, there is nothing. We have commented on this before. The argument that the material may not have been available in early August might have had some slight relevance.

The chronology might have been the vehicle for addressing this shortcoming. However, fully two months later, there is still nothing included of the enemy's C3I – the huge gap is not addressed, much less explained, by NSA.

(S//SI) Over the years, the chronology came to be the source book for responses to congressional inquiries into the Gulf of Tonkin incidents. That is, the other 90 percent of related SIGINT product was not offered to any congressional investigating committees. Instead, the chronology became, by virtue of its position as an "official" report, the only source for background on the Gulf of Tonkin incidents.

(TS//SI) The first investigation came in early 1968 when the Senate Foreign Relations Committee, under the chairmanship of Senator William Fulbright, who had steered the Gulf of Tonkin Resolution through the Senate, opened hearings on the incident. Secretary of Defense Robert McNamara was called in to testify. Prior to his testimony, he requested that the pertinent COMINT on the incidents be given to him. The NSA and the Defense Intelligence Agency were reluctant to have the SIGINT used; both agencies were fearful that the exposure would compromise the then current capabilities against the North Vietnamese.[182] Ultimately, Secretary McNamara was given the contents of the chronology, as was the Senate committee as well. The resulting hearings did nothing to clear up the confusion. McNamara argued for the attack, citing the various SIGINT reports, though he seemed to mix up what was in them, and left observers sometimes confused.[183] Many senators, looking at the same chronology, remained skeptical.

(S//SI) In August 1975, the Senate Select Committee on Intelligence, under the chairmanship of Senator Frank Church of Idaho, approached NSA about the Gulf of Tonkin incident. The committee's interest, though, may not have been in establishing the validity of the incident; their attention was focused on information concerning the covert OPLAN 34A and Desoto missions, and what exactly was being done by both operations. NSA's response to the Church Committee's request was similar to that of Fulbright's: limited release of materials from the chronology. In fact, NSA was concerned that the Church Committee get exactly what Fulbright had received.[184] Again, the chronology of the events of 2 to 4 August was the source used for material to be released. Interestingly, a major figure in these latter deliberations on what to release to the Senate was the then-retired, former deputy director of NSA, Dr. Louis Tordella. He had advised the NSA staff as to what to release and hold back. Curiously, one of the few things held back was a similar chronology of the events of mid-September 1964, in which another Desoto patrol claimed it had been attacked.

(S//SI) Gulf of Tonkin Redux: The 18 September "Attack"

(S//SI) In an interesting and ironic repeat of the Gulf of Tonkin incidents, on 18 September 1964 another Desoto patrol would undergo the same experience as the *Maddox* and *Turner Joy*. In this incident, two destroyers, the USS *Morton* (DD 948) and the USS *Richard S. Edwards* (DD 950), were assigned a Desoto mission for mid-September. The ships began their operations on 16 September. The North Vietnamese knew almost from the start that the two vessels would be in the area and were tracking it. The DRV naval authorities also ordered their ships and posts to be on alert and to be aware for "provocations" by the Americans.[185]

(S//SI) North Vietnamese tracking of the two destroyers held through the 17th and into the 18th of September. At 1738G (1038Z) on 18 September, a message was passed from an unidentified DRV naval authority that ordered all ships to take precautions against possible South Vietnamese maritime commandos who might take advantage of the presence of the American ships in the area to launch an attack. The North

Vietnamese ships were also ordered to "avoid provocation" and to disperse and camouflage.[186]

(U) At about 1729G (1029Z), the two destroyers acquired radar contacts following them. Both ships began to maneuver and increase speed to clear the apparent vessels trailing them. About forty-five minutes later, the *Morton* fired a warning shot at one of the contacts. By this time, the Americans counted on their radar scopes five ships trailing them. However, the warning shot did not deter the threatening vessels. About ten minutes later, both ships opened fire. For about the next hour, both American ships engaged the contacts as they appeared on their radar screens. Oddly, at no time did the contacts return any fire, nor did they launch any torpedoes. Even more curious, only one of the enemy ships ever closed faster than twenty-three knots. In fact, the contacts pretty much matched the speeds of the destroyers. Meanwhile, the *Morton* and *Edwards* fired almost 300 rounds at the contacts and claimed to sink as many as five of the vessels (there were now more than the original five contacts) which had been menacing them.

(S) The JCS ordered a search, to begin the next morning, of the area for debris to confirm the attacks. At the same time, plans were put under way for another retaliatory strike against the DRV. More air force and navy aircraft were dispatched to the region to reinforce the proposed strikes.[187] Yet, nothing happened. The area was searched, but no debris nor even an oil slick was found. The JCS continued to request data on the attacks from all the intelligence and combat commands. Yet even by the 19th there still was no concrete evidence of an attack.[188]

(TS//SI) Available SIGINT information indicated that the North Vietnamese were well aware of the presence of the two destroyers, but remained in a defensive posture. The DRV was looking to react to a possible maritime raid by the South Vietnamese, but there were no reflections of any hostile intent against the two destroyers.[189] In fact, on 20 September NSA corrected a Critic by San Miguel which claimed that the DRV was planning to attack the Desoto patrol that evening. Fort Meade pointed out that the intercepted information could apply equally to an attack on South Vietnamese "raiders."[190]

(U) By the end of 20 September, the issue remained unresolved. The *Edwards* and *Morton* were ordered to return to the nearby carrier task group, and the Desoto missions were indefinitely suspended, and, in fact, except for an occasional training cruise, they were never carried out again.[191]

*   *   *   *

(U) In certain histories of the Indochina War, it has been fashionable to maintain that, in the final accounting, whether or not there was an attack on U.S. Navy destroyers on 4 August in the Gulf of Tonkin may not have mattered at all. The Johnson administration had been looking for a way to expand America's role in South Vietnam. In June 1964, two months before the August attacks, a resolution had been prepared by William Bundy, assistant secretary of state for Far Eastern Affairs, which would give the president the right to commit U.S. forces to the defense of any nation in Southeast Asia threatened by communist aggression or subversion. Furthermore, the draft resolution gave Johnson both the discretion to determine the extent of the threat and, by virtue of this evaluation, the leeway to define what forces and actions were necessary to counter it. At first, the resolution was planned to be put before the Senate as soon as possible. But President Johnson demurred, fearing that it would ruin the image of moderation he had been cultivating for the presidential election in November. The draft resolution was quietly shelved until another opportunity could come along.[192]

(U) The Johnson administration used the 4 August incident to ride the resurrected resolution, now popularly referred to as the Tonkin Gulf Resolution, through the Senate, with only two dissenting votes. It was portrayed as a moderating measure "calculated to prevent the spread of war."[193] However, President Johnson now had the legal cover to use whatever military force he wanted. When he heard of its passage by both houses, he laughed and told an aide that the resolution "was like Grandma's nightshirt. It covers everything."[194]

(U) Yet, even with the resolution in his pocket, President Johnson ignored the similar September Gulf of Tonkin "incident," and did not order a retaliation against North Vietnam. It would take another communist attack on American forces, the strike at the American base at Pleiku in February 1965, to make Washington escalate the war a further step, this time initiating the Rolling Thunder air campaign.[195]

(U) The problem, of course, was the nature of the provocation which made possible the passage of the resolution. If the resolution had been tied to the naval action of the afternoon of 2 August, or to the communist bombing of the officers' quarters in Saigon on Christmas Eve 1964, or even to the VC sapper attack on the air base at Bien Hoa on 1 November 1964, then the administration at least would have had an actual incident upon which to base support for it. Then any reconsideration of the resolution would have centered solely on it and not the incident on which it was based.

(U) Unfortunately, the administration chose to hang the rationale for expanding its war-making franchise in Southeast Asia on an incident which could not stand up to any kind of objective examination of the full documentation. So, as eventually happened in 1968, when the Gulf of Tonkin Resolution came to be reviewed, the incident that it was based on also came under scrutiny. When the events of 4 August were revealed to have been based on very thin evidence, it concurrently was demonstrated that the Johnson administration had indulged in a very selective use of information. If the administration had not lied exactly, it had not been exactly honest with the public, or, for that matter, even honest within its own deliberations. The question no longer was about the appropriateness of the resolution, but the basic honesty of the administration. It would cast a pall on an already distrusted Johnson presidency. As Senator Barry Goldwater, who had run against Johnson in the 1964 presidential election, bitterly noted years later in 1972, "I had no reason to believe that Mr. Johnson's account of the gravity existing in the Gulf of Tonkin was not legitimate." [196]

(U) As for the Tonkin Gulf incident itself, President Johnson summed it up best just a few days later: "Hell, those damn, stupid sailors were just shooting at flying fish."

*   *   *   *

(U) In this article we have done something quite apart from most Agency histories: Using virtually hitherto untouched material from a variety of sources, we have told a radically different version of an important event in cryptologic history which, in turn, had a critical effect on the course of American history. In doing so, a great deal of unfamiliar ground, in terms of source material, had to be covered, and the new information could not be presented in a typical, historical narrative format. Instead, we had to painstakingly analyze a series of documents which were quite important if we were to grasp what happened on 4 August 1964. Admittedly, this was a difficult task, but it was necessary if we were to be as comprehensive as possible in our analysis of what happened.

(U) After recounting all of the events and analyzing the sources, the remaining task for the historian is to attempt to characterize them, to offer a summation or a judgment that will place the narrative into a coherent framework. But before that can be done, it is necessary to review what has been presented. In this way we can consider again what we have learned about the events in early August.

(S//SI) We have seen that the Gulf of Tonkin incidents occurred as a result of the congruence of the Desoto patrols and the maritime commando raids along the North Vietnamese coast carried out under OPLAN 34A. In the period leading up to the *Maddox* mission, the DRV had been reacting with increasing force to the OPLAN 34A attacks. Monitoring Hanoi's more aggressive response to the raids, NSA had warned the major commands in the region of the potential danger for the Desoto patrols, but the warning did not register. The decision makers in Washington

(U) A Douglas A-4 Skyhawk attack plane catapults from a carrier in the Gulf of Tonkin during attack operations in August 1964.

believed that Hanoi would not see the two missions as related.

(S//SI) On 2 August, the SIGINT system performed admirably when it provided sufficient warning to the *Maddox* to allow it to defend itself against the attack by the three DRV torpedo boats. At the same time, the American cryptologists were able to observe the DRV naval C3I system in action. From this they should have developed a profile from which further timely warnings could be deduced. During 3 August, both sides maintained a distant watchfulness, though tensions remained high – high enough, perhaps, for the field site at Phu Bai to confuse salvage operations around the island of Hon Me for a pre-attack concentration of forces.

(S//SI) The 4 August incident began in the early afternoon due to an analytic error by the Marine contingent at Phu Bai. This mistake set in the minds of the crew of the two destroyers the idea that they shortly would be attacked. This was an error of interpretation by the Marine unit at Phu Bai, a mistake, as we have seen, which was not committed by the navy site at San Miguel. Nor was the Critic transmitted by Phu Bai questioned or corrected at NSA. This may have been in line with an unspoken policy of not second-guessing field sites since they were "closer" to the action. However, under Critic procedures, Phu Bai had to supply the technical information upon which it based its alert. When the discrepancy between what the intercept actually said and what the Marine detachment reported became known, NSA should have cautioned the recipients of the Critic. However, this did not happen.

(S//SI) Three hours later, at almost the same moment that the American destroyers opened fire on the approaching radar return, Phu Bai issued another report which stated that the specific boats, which had been identified as being readied for an attack, in reality, were to be towed to Haiphong for repairs. This salvage operation would be the subject of several more reports dur-

ing the rest of the evening of 4 August. Since no other boats were referenced in the original "attack" message, the cryptologists at NSA found themselves without any SIGINT evidence supporting the reports of an ambush. The Phu Bai reports had effectively cancelled out the original Critic. However, the response by NSA was to counter the SIGINT evidence with an unfounded speculation that the boats the Desoto patrol thought were attacking it came from Quang Khe. And it has been demonstrated how impossible this scenario was.

(S//SI) It also has been established that none of the C3I associated with DRV naval attack of 2 August was present on 4 August. Aside from sporadic North Vietnamese coastal tracking, which ended hours before the two destroyers turned east, there was no intercept to suggest the North Vietnamese had anything more than the usual interest in the two ships. Nor, for that matter, was there any intercept of any DRV naval communications which suggested in any manner that an attack was planned, much less that one actually was occurring. In fact, Hanoi seemed more interested in warning its boats of the patrol's presence, viewing the Americans as a threat to its navy. For the cryptologic community, this lack of any attack C3I is one of the most critical points of the Gulf of Tonkin crisis. Yet, NSA never addressed the issue in any reports or activity summaries it published concerning the 4 August incident.

(S//SI) Instead, NSA would issue summaries with scattered tidbits of contentious and unreferenced intercept ("Khoai had met the enemy" and the purported aerial tracking) to support the notion that an attack had been planned and that it had been carried out. The extensive amount of SIGINT evidence that contradicted both the initial attack order and the notion that any North Vietnamese boats were involved in any "military operations," other than salvage of the two damaged torpedo boats, was either misrepresented or excluded from all NSA produced post-incident summaries, reports, or chronologies. NSA's failure to deal with both issues, the lack of any attack C3I and the contradictory SIGINT, especially during the critical hours leading up to the retaliatory air strikes of 5 August, remains its most glaring shortcoming in this incident.

(S//SI) We have seen as well the many technical problems with the supposed "after-action" translation. This product, upon which the administration based so much of its case, appears to have been the result of an analytic error of combining two separate messages, each dealing with separate incidents, into a single translation. There were more problems, such as the actual translation of the term "comrades" and how it was rendered into "boats" by NSA. Here, the analytic problems mix with those discovered about the available records: the original decrypted Vietnamese text, and an important translation from San Miguel cannot be located. Considering the importance of this translation to the administration's case, the fact that the original text cannot be found (and was not used as early as October 1964) is unusual. That these original texts and translation are the only missing papers in the San Miguel reports allows for suspicion to shade any further discourses.

(S//SI) What we are confronted with is the same conundrum that confronted the NSA analysts at the time. We have discussed earlier that, for the most part, the NSA personnel in the crisis center who reported the second Gulf of Tonkin incident believed that it had occurred. The problem for them was the SIGINT evidence. The evidence that supported the contention that an attack had occurred was scarce and nowhere as strong as would have been wanted. The overwhelming body of reports, if used, would have told the story that no attack had happened. So a conscious effort ensued to demonstrate that the attack occurred.

(S//SI) The exact "how" and "why" for this effort to provide only the SIGINT that supported the claim of an attack remain unknown. There are no "smoking gun" memoranda or notes buried in the files that outline any plan or state a justification. Instead, the paper record speaks for itself on what happened: what few product (six) were actually used, and how 90 percent of them were kept out of the chronology; how contradictory SIGINT evidence was answered both with speculation and fragments lifted from context; how the complete lack of Vietnamese C3I was not addressed; and, finally, how critical original Vietnamese text and subsequent product were no longer available. From this evidence, one can easily deduce the deliberate nature of these actions. And this observation makes sense, for there was a purpose to them: This was an active effort to make SIGINT fit the claim of what happened during the evening of 4 August in the Gulf of Tonkin.

(S//SI) The question why the NSA personnel handled the product the way they did will probably never be answered. The notion that they were under "pressure" to deliver the story that the administration wanted simply cannot be supported. If the participants are to be believed, and they were adamant in asserting this, they did not bend to the desires of administration officials. Also, such "environmental" factors as overworked crisis center personnel and lack of experienced linguists are, for the most part, not relevant when considering the entire period of the crisis and follow-up. As we have seen, the efforts to ensure that the only SIGINT publicized would be that which supported the contention that an attack had occurred continued long after the crisis had passed. While the product initially issued on the 4 August incident may be contentious, thin, and mistaken, what was issued in the Gulf of Tonkin summaries beginning late on 4 August was deliberately skewed to support the notion that there had been an attack. What was placed in the official chronology was even more selective. That the NSA personnel believed that the attack happened and rationalized the contradictory evidence away is probably all that is necessary to know in order to understand what was done. They walked alone in their counsels.

(b)(3)-P.L. 86-36

(U) Notes

1. (U) James S. Olson and Randy Roberts, *Where the Domino Fell: America and Vietnam 1945 to 1990* (New York: St Martin's Press, 1991), 118.

2. (U) James Bond and Sybil Stockdale, *In Love and War* (New York: Harper & Row, 1984), 19.

3. (U) Robert S. McNamara, *In Retrospect: The Tragedy and Lessons of Vietnam* (New York: Time Books, 1995), 134-135. However, in the introduction to the paperback edition of *In Retrospect*, McNamara pulls back a bit from his traditional certainty.

4. (U) Edward J. Marolda and Oscar P. Fitzgerald, *The United States Navy and the Vietnam Conflict, Vol II: From Military Assistance to Combat, 1959-1965* (Washington, D.C.: Naval Historical Center, 1986), 440-442.

5. (U) Edwin Moise, *Tonkin Gulf and the Escalation of the Vietnam War* (Chapel Hill, NC: University of North Carolina Press, 1996), 199-200.

6. (TS//SI [   ] The Gulf of Tonkin Incident," *Cryptolog*, February-March 1975, 8-10; "Tonkin Gulf: The Untold Story of the 'Phantom Battle' that Led to War," *U.S. News and World Report*, July 23, 1984, 84. (S//SI) The source of this quote was a 20 January 1972 meeting between the Deputy Director NSA, Dr. Louis Tordella, and the Chief of Staff, Senate Foreign Relations Committee, Carl Marcy. In that meeting Dr. Tordella conceded that the intercept of 4 August could refer to the 2 August attack. Dr. Tordella could not produce the "original" version of the report in question. "Reading file of the Deputy Director," July-December 1971, NCA ACC# 25853 and similar file, January-July 1972, NCA ACC# 25854.

7. (U) Marolda, 442.

8. (U) McNamara, 134; Lyndon B. Johnson, *Vantage Point: Perspectives of the Presidency 1963-1969* (New York: Holt Rinehart and Winston, 1971), 114-115.

9. (U) McNamara, 130.

10. (U) Marolda, 394-395.

11. (U) Ibid., 395.

12. (U) McNamara, 130.

13. (U) Marolda, 398.

14. (U) Ibid., 404.

15. (TS//SI) William Gerhard, *In the Shadow of War (To the Gulf of Tonkin)*, Cryptologic History Series, Southeast Asia, June 1969, National Security Agency, 51.

16. (TS//SI) OIC USN-467 Yankee. "SIGINT Operations Report, Desoto February/March Patrol, Submission of," 23 August 1961, NSG Archives, Box 7 file 32316. Direct Support Operations Pacific 1964; 2/O/VHN/T01-64, 021943Z March 1964.

17. (TS//SI) Gerhard, 51. Naval DSUs used the SIGAD USN-467 as a generic designator for their missions. Each specific patrol received a letter suffix for its duration. The next mission would receive the subsequent letter in an alphabetic sequence.

18. (S//SI) HQ NSAPAC to DIRNSA, 262020Z August 1964.

19. (TS//SI) USN-27, "Standard Operating Procedures for Support of August 1964 Desoto Patrol," 28 July 1964.

20. (S) CINCPAC, 140203Z July 1964.

21. (S) Ibid.

22. (TS//SI) See 3/O/VHK/T24-60, 20 July 1960 and 3/O/VHM/T10-60, 28 July 1960, among others.

23. 2/G9/VHM/R28-64, 10 June 1964, inter alia; see *Secret Army, Secret War* by S. Tourison for a complete recounting of these doomed missions.

24. (S//SI) NSACSS MACV, [   ] /Tiger, 6 (b)(1) (b)(3)

25. (S//SI) Ibid., Appendix A-1.

26. (S//SI) Ibid., A-2.

27. (S//SI) Ibid., A-3.

28. (U) Harold P. Ford, *CIA and the Vietnam Policymakers: Three Episodes, 1962-1968* (Center for the Study of Intelligence, Central Intelligence Agency, 1998), 46.

29. (U) McNamara, 133; Moise, 22.

30. (U) Olson and Roberts, 117.

31. (U) Moise, 25; Young, 115.

32. (S//SI) 2/Q/VHN/T13-64, 281006Z July 1964.

33. (S//SI) 2/Q/VHN/T76-64, 010652Z July 1964.

34. (S//SI) 2/O/VHN/R03-64, 8 June 1964.

35. (U) Moise, 25.

36. (TS//SI) Gerhard, 112; also, see DIRNSA 08006/02, 021615Z August 1964.

per CIA

(b)(3)-P.L. 86-36

37. (TS//SI) Oral History interview with [REDACTED] Navy enlisted Vietnamese linguist, 22 December 1987, NSA OH 33-87, 8; Oral History interview with Lieutenant General Gordon A. Blake USAF, Director NSA, 1962-1965, 5 June 1972, NSA OH -72, 5 June 1972, 3-4.

38. (TS//SI) DIRNSA, 070118Z August 1964.

39. (S//SI) 2/Q/VHN/R24-64, 310922Z July 1964.

40. (TS//SI) [REDACTED] OH 33-87.

41. (S//SI) 2/G11/VHN/R01-64 Spot Report, 011635Z August 1964; (TS//SI) OIC USN 467 November. "July-August 1964 Desoto Patrol SIGINT Operations Report," Serial 0003, 23 August 1964.

42. (S//SI) 2/Q/VHN/T26-64, 01924Z August 1964; 2/Q/VHN/T137-64, 080216Z August 1964.

43. (S//SI) 2/Q/VHN/T130-64, 050827Z August 1964.

44. (S//SI) 2/Q/VHN/R27-64, 012152Z August 1964; FLWP Nr.1 to 2/Q/VHN/R27-64.

45. (S//SI) 2/G11/VHN/R02-64, 020745Z August 1964.

46. (S//SI) DIRNSA. "Possible Planned Attack by DRV Navy on Desoto Patrol," B205/981-64, 020302Z August 1964; NSA Command Center Record of Events, 2 August 1964. The navy intercept site [REDACTED] had the responsibility for relaying Criticomm messages to the DSU aboard the *Maddox*. However, the initial Critic for 2 August was NOT passed until much later. NCA ACC# 45582, H04-0301-4.

47. (S//SI) CRITIC, USN-27 to DIRNSA, 020444Z August 1964; 2/G11/VHN/R02-64, 020745Z August 1964.

48. (S//SI) Ibid.

49. (S//SI) 2/G11/VHN/R06-64, 022127Z August 1964.

50. (S//SI) 2/Q/VHN/T135-64 050950Z August 1964.

51. (U) Moise, 73.

52. (S//SI) 2/Q/VHN/T134-64 050948Z August 1964.

53. (S//SI) 2/G11/R03-64, 020822Z August 1964.

54. (U) Moise, 73.

55. (U) Ibid., 74.

56. (TS//SI) DIRNSA, 020947Z August 1964, 08004/02.

57. (U) Moise, 84.

58. (U) Ibid., 86; (S//SI) 2/G11/VHN/R10-64 040850Z August 1964.

59. (S//SI) 2/G11/VHN/R08-64, 031925Z.

60. (S//SI) 2/G11/VHN/R10-64, 040850Z August 1964.

61. (U) Marolda, 421.

62. (U) Moise, 88; Marolda, 415.

63. (U) McNamara, 140-141.

64. (TS) Marshall Wright, et al., "The Vietnam Information Group. Presidential Decisions: The Gulf of Tonkin Attacks of August 1964," Lyndon B. Johnson Library, 1 November 1968, CCH Series VIII Box 13.

65. (TS//SI) DIRNSA. "DRV Vessels Attack Desoto Patrol in Gulf of Tonkin," B205/243-64 020947Z August 1964.

66. (TS//SI) DIRNSA, 021628Z, 3/O/[REDACTED] R15-64.

67. (S) CINCPACFLT, 021104Z August 1964.

68. (S) CTU 72.1.2, 021443Z (Genser).

69. (S) Desoto OPSUM, 021443Z August 1964.

70. (TS) Wright, 12.

71. (S//SI) 2/Q/VHN/T126-64, 030450Z August 1964.

72. (S//SI) 2/Q/VHN/T131-64, 050834Z August 1964.

73. (S//SI) 2/G11/VHN/R07-64 August 1964.

74. (S) July/August Desoto SITSUM (3) 030745Z August 1964 GENSER.

75. (S//SI) 2/Q/VHN/R32-64 031008Z August 1964.

76. (S//SI) 2/Q/VHN/T144-64 080234Z August 1964.

77. (S//SI) 2/Q/VHN/T142-64 080228Z August 1964; (U) Marolda, 421.

78. (TS//SI) OIC USN-467N, July-August 1964 Desoto Patrol SIGINT Observations Report," USNSGA Ser 0003 23 August 1964.

79. (U) Marolda, 423; (S) CTG 72.1 "July-August Desoto SITSUM," 031405Z August 1964; (S//SI) 2/Q/VHN/R32-64 031008Z August 1964.

80. (S//SI) 2/Q/VHN/T146-64 080314Z August 1964.

81. (S//SI) 2/Q/VHN/T151-64 080324Z August 1964.

(b)(1)
(b)(3)-50 USC 403
(b)(3)-P.L. 86-36

TOP SECRET//COMINT//X1

(b)(1)
(b)(3)-50 USC 403
(b)(3)-18 USC 798
(b)(3)-P.L. 86-36

Page 51

Body-52

82. (S//SI) Critic USN-414T, 041115Z August 1964.

83. (S//SI) 2/G11/VHN/R11-64, 041140Z, August 1964.

84. (S) CTU 77.12, 041240Z.

85. (S//SI) An interesting speculation emerged after Captain Herrick's initial radar contact placed the suspect boats so far to the northeast of his position that these craft could have been Chinese Communist naval vessels on patrol from nearby Hainan Island. As

86. (U) Moise, 123.

87. (U) Moise, 127; Marolda, 429.

88. (U) Moise, 71.

89. (U) Ibid., 126.

90. (U) Ibid., 127.

91. (U) Joseph C. Goulden, *Truth is the First Casualty* (New York: James B. Adler Inc., 1969), 146.

92. (U) Ibid., 143.

93. (U) Moise, 129, 160.

94. (U) Goulden, 144.

95. (U) Moise, 144.

96. (S) Desoto Action SITREP, Z 041754Z August 1964.

97. (S) CTU 77.12 "Attack on Desoto Final SITREP," 042158 August 1964, CCH Series VII. Box 13.

98. (U) Moise, 211-212; Robert Divine, *Since 1945: Politics and Diplomacy in Recent American History* (New York: Alfred Knoff, 1985 (Third edition)), 139.

99. (U) Moise, 209; John Schulzinger, *A Time for War: The United States and Vietnam, 1941-1975* (New York: Oxford University Press, 1997), 151.

100. (S) "Memorandum for Mr. Bundy," 23, 10 August 1964 from LBJ Library, CCH Series VIII, Box 13, Gulf of Tonkin, "Vietnam War Records."

101. (S) Ibid.

102. (S) CTU 77.12 Desoto, Final SITREP, Z 042158Z August 1964.

103. (S) CTG 77.5, Desoto Patrol SITREP Nr 8., Z 041928Z August 1964.

104. (S//SI) 2/O/VHN/T10-64, 041559Z August 1964; also, portions quoted in 3/0/VHN/R01-64.

105. (S) "Memorandum for Mr. Bundy," 24; McNamara, 134.

106. (U) Lyndon B. Johnson, 114-115.

107. (TS//SI) 3/O/VHN/R01-64, 5 August 1964.

108. (S//SI) USN-414T, 041115Z August 1964.

109. (S//SI) USM-626J, 041140Z August 1964.

110. (S//SI) 2/G11/VHN/R13-64, 041440Z August 1964. It is possible that this intercept was the missing part of the message sent earlier and construed as the "attack" order.

111. (S//SI) 2/Q/VHN/T163-64, 090328Z August 1964.

112. (S//SI) 2/G11/VHN/R17-64, 041820Z August 1964.

113. (S//SI) 2/Q/VHN/R42-64, 041900Z August 1964.

114. (S) CTU 77.12 Z 041240Z August 1964.

115. (S//SI) 2/Q/VHN/T128-64 041838Z August 1964.

116. (S//SI) Ibid.

117. (TS//SI) 3/O/VHN/R01-64, 5 August 1964.

118. (U) Marolda, 408; bomb damage assessments from 5 August indicate that some P-4s may have been at Quang Khe. However, there is no SIGINT reflection to support any activity during this period by P-4s in the Southern Naval Command.

119. (S//SI) 2/G11/VHN/R16-64, 041746Z August 1964.

120. (S) JCS Z O 041628Z August 1964, CCH Series VI.HH.24.10.

121. (S//SI) 2/G11/VHN/R15-64, 041745Z August 1964.

122. (S//SI) DIRNSA, 070118Z August 1964.

123. (S//SI) US-467N, 070615Z, August 1964.

124. (S//SI) 2/Q/VHN/T151-64, 080324Z August 1964. NCA ACC# 45359Z.

125. (S//SI) 2/Q/VHN/T152-64, 080440Z August 1964, NCA ACC# 45359Z.

126. (S//SI) 2/O/VHN/R11-64, Spot Report 3 September 1964.

127. (S//SI) Ibid.

128. (S//SI) OIC, USN-467N.

129. (S//SI) Ibid.

130. (TS//SI) COMNAVFORJAPAN. "Preliminary All Source Evaluation Maddox Patrol," 120230Z October 1964.

131. (U) Moise, 163-164.

132. (U) Sir Arthur Conan Doyle, *The Complete Sherlock Holmes* (Garden City, New York: Doubleday & Company, 1930), 347.

133. (U) Moise, 201.

134. (U) OIC USN-467N.

135. (S//SI) 2/Q/VHN/T126-64, 030450Z August 1964; attached worksheet 1609-64, USN-414T. NCA ACC# 45359Z, USN-27 1964 translations. Also, see 2/G11/VHN/R06-64, 022127Z August 1964.

136. (S//SI) 2/Q/VHN/R39-64, 041646Z August 1964. This serialized report was sent at a precedence ("ZZ") reserved for Critics. This was a technical error and did not affect warning or timeliness. However, it makes tracking down the reports more difficult.

137. (U) Moise, 200.

138. (S//SI) B26 COMINT Technical Report #009-65, [ ] 29 March 1965, CCH Series XII.NN.

139. (U) Moise, 200; Lyndon B. Johnson, 114. (TS//SI) In the matter of who the "experts" were that President Johnson is referring to, it appears that they were members of the White House Intelligence Advisory Staff. According to one source, they examined "all available intelligence having even the most remote relevance [to the Gulf of Tonkin]." According to this source, SIGINT alone provided "positive evidence of DRV premeditation." Whether this evidence refers to the 2 or 4 August incidents is unclear. It is also not certain if all "relevant intelligence" was pursued. Furthermore, it is not clear if any of the "experts" were Vietnamese linguists, or if they were being prompted by the analysts at NSA. Source: NSA Memorandum for the Record: "Interview with Mr. Arthur McCafferty, White House Staff, on the use of SIGINT in Shaping White House Decisions on Southeast Asia," CCH Series XII.NN., undated.

140. (S//SI) 2/Q/VHN/R39-64.

141. (S//SI) For identity of LAP, see 2/Q/VHN/T123-64; for TRA see 2/Q/VHN/T134, 135-64. Callwords/covernames were used to designate units, entities, and individuals. It was not uncommon to see

a particular entity, such as T-142, addressed with as many as three callwords over this period. However, these callwords equated to any number of differing entities that would have been aboard.

142. (S//SI) The missing intercept would have arrived in the form of so-called technical supplements to the San Miguel reports "38" and "39." Generally these supplements were sent anywhere from fifteen to forty-five minutes after the report was issued. They included the original Vietnamese text. These supplements were sent to a small audience of SIGINT-producing elements. The supplements probably were what the B26 crisis center used in generating the after-action report, "T-10."

(S//SI) As a general practice, once the technical supplements were received, they were attached to the original reports. A review of the NSA archival file containing the San Miguel reports issued in 1964 revealed that reports in the preceding and following series have their supplements attached, while the two reports in questions stand alone, *sans* supplements.

143. (S//SI) 2/Q/VHN/T163-64, 080522Z August 1964; as reported in 2/Q/VHN/R38-64, 041632Z August 1964. The text of "R38" was "at 041554Z *Swatow*-class PGM T-142 reported to My Duc (19°52'N, 105°57'E) that an enemy aircraft was observed falling into the sea. Enemy vessel perhaps wounded." The translation quoted on page 34 was of the full text that would have appeared in the missing Technical Supplement.

144. (S//SI) Ibid.

145. (U) Moise, 106.

146. (S//SI) 2/G11/VHN/R10-64, 040850Z August 1964.

147. (U) Moise, 199-200.

148. (TS//SI) Oral History interview with [ ] [ ] 13. Oral History interview with Lieutenant General Gordon Blake, 4.

149. (TS//SI) Blake Oral History, 9.

150. (U) Moise, 197.

151. (TS//SI) Johnson, 522.

152. (TS//SI) [ ] Oral History; Oral History Interview with Milt Zaslow, OH 17-93.

153. (S//SI) [ ] Oral History.

154. (S//SI) Ibid.

155. (TS//SI) See 3/O/VHN/R01-64, Spot Report 4 August 1964; 3/O/VHN/R02-64, 060102Z August 1964; and 3/O/VHN/R03-64, 061604Z August 1964.

156. (TS//SI) _____ Oral History, 8; Zaslow Oral History, 33-35.

157. (TS//SI) Blake Oral History, 12.

158. (U) Moise, 241-243.

159. (S//SI) HQ NSAPAC 080105Z August 1964; William Gerhard, Untitled Notes on Gulf of Tonkin, CCH Series XII.NN (1970).

160. (U) Marolda, 443.

161. (TS//SI) DIRNSA File, "Gulf of Tonkin, Both Incidents," CCH Series VI.24.6.

162. (TS//SI) OIC USN-467N.

163. (S//SI) DIRNAVSECGRUPAC 241832Z August 1963.

164. (S//SI) 2/O/VHN/T11-64, 061656Z August 1964. A curious archival sidenote to this translation. When this historian reviewed the original NCA accession of NSA-issued translations of DRV naval intercept, this one translation was missing. A copy was found in the files on the Tonkin Gulf incidents held by the Center for Cryptologic History. A copy was then replaced in the NCA file.

165. (TS//SI) 3/O/VHN/R01-64, 050130Z August 1964 NCA ACC# 45359Z.

166. (S) See the following: JCS messages, 041610Z August 1964; 041830Z August 1964; 041811Z August 1964; and 041754Z August 1964, Desoto Action Sitrep.

167. (TS//SI) Spot Report 3/O/VHN/R03-64 August 1964 NCA ACC# 45359Z.

168. (TS//SI) NSA Command Center record of Events, 6 August 1964, NCA ACC# 45582.

169. (TS//SI) 3/O/VHN/R01-64.

170. (TS//SI) 3/O/VHN/R01-64, 5 August 1964.

171. (S//SI) 2/Q/VHS/R36-64 031212Z August 1964; USN-27 Tech Supplement to same, 031236Z August 1964.

172. (S//SI) Ibid. Also, Desoto SITSUM 5, 030745Z Genser August 1964; and 3/O/VHS/R38-64 DRV MERSUM 3-9 August 1964.

173. (S//SI) Ibid.

174. (TS//SI) Spot Report 3/O/VHN/#03-64, 6 August 1964.

175. (TS//SI) Blake Oral History, 7.

176. (S//SI) 2/Q/VHN/T154-64, 080328Z August 1964.

177. (U) Moise, 78.

178. (S//SI) DIRNSA File, Gulf of Tonkin, Both Incidents, CCH Series VI.24.6.

179. (TS//SI) Lt. Col. Delmar Lang USAF, "Chronology of Events of 2-5 August 1964 in the Gulf of Tonkin," 14 October 1964, CCH Series VI.HH.24.10.

180. (TS//SI) Ibid., paragraph 8.

181. (TS//SI) They are, in order: 2/G11/VHN/R07-64, 030956Z August 1964; USN-414T Critic, 041115Z August 1964; 2/G11/VHN/R11-64, 041140Z August 1964; USN-414T Translation, unnumbered (time of intercept 040927Z August 1964); 2/O/VHN/T10-64, 041955Z August 1964; and 2/G11/VHN/R18-64, 050435Z August 1964.

182. (TS//SI) Memorandum for the Secretary of Defense, "Release of COMINT Pertaining to Gulf of Tonkin Incidents of 2 and 4 August 1964," SI-TS-61/PL-4, 13 December 1967, CCH Series VIII, Box 13, Gulf of Tonkin Incident.

183. (TS//SI) Blake Oral History, 12. (U) Washington Post, 25 February 1968, "McNamara Describes Gulf of Tonkin Incident." At separate times Secretary McNamara refers to four, then nine COMINT Reports in his testimony.

184. (U) Note, Bill Gerhard to Mr. Lowman, et al., Subject: "Following for information concerning request/response," 3 September 1975, CCH Series VIII, Box 13, Gulf of Tonkin Incident.

185. (S//SI) 2/Q1/VHN/R10-64, 170515Z September 1964. NCA ACC# 45349Z.

186. (S//SI) 2/Q1/VHN/R18-64, 180920Z September 1964.

187. (S) JCS, 190309Z September 1964.

188. (S) JCS, 190536Z September 1964.

189. (TS//SI) B205, "Chronology of Events of 18-20 September 1964 in the Gulf of Tonkin," 14 January 1965, 4. After the second incident in September, the difference in the NSA reporting, that is, the lack of evidence for an attack, was noted quickly by the PFIAB. This led the Board to order an investigation, which, in turn, led to the development of the chronologies of the two attacks. Blake Oral History, 10-12, 14.

190. (TS//SI) Ibid., 5.

190. (TS//SI) Ibid., 5.

191. (U) Marolda and Fitzgerald, 462.

192. (U) Olson and Roberts, 117; Schulzinger, 148.

193. (U) Karnow, 376.

194. (U) Olson and Roberts, 120.

195. (U) The Gulf of Tonkin Resolution was repealed in May 1970. Ironically, the initiative for the repeal originated with Senator Robert Dole of Kansas.

196. (U) *Congressional Record*, Volume 118, Part 3, 92nd Congress, 2nd Session, 3-14 February 1972, 3313.

(U//FOUO) Mr. Hanyok is a senior historian with the Center for Cryptologic History (E05). He worked in the NSA/CSS Archives from 1992 to 1994 and in the National SIGINT Operations Center from 1990 to 1992. Mr. Hanyok has also served as a collection officer in G Group (1976-1979), in the COMSEC Doctrine organization (1979-1982), as a Traffic Analysis intern (1982-1984), and as an analyst in A Group (1984-1990). He holds the title of master in the technical track program of the Intelligence Analysis Career field.